Lifelong Diplomat

by
R. Richard Rubottom, Jr.

As told to
Janis Williams

FIRST EDITION
Copyright © 2011
By R. Richard Rubottom, Jr.
Printed in the United States of America
By Nortex Press
A Division of Sunbelt Media, Inc.
P.O. Box 21235 ▢ Waco, Texas 76702
email: sales@eakinpress.com
▢ website: www.eakinpress.com ▢
ALL RIGHTS RESERVED.
1 2 3 4 5 6 7 8 9
ISBN 13: 978-1-935632-12-2
ISBN 10: 1-935632-12-4
Library of Congress Control Number 2010942149

Contents

Introduction   v

PART ONE

Chapter

1: 1912–1928   3
2: 1928–1938 12
3: 1938–1946 25

PART TWO

4: 1946–1948 37
5: 1950–1951 60
6: 1951–1952 68
7: 1953–1956 74
8: 1956–1961 91
9: In His Own Words: Reflections on Cuba 107
10: A Diplomatic Tour of South America, 1958. . . . 145
11: Becoming an Ambassador. 169
12: Naval War College, 1961–1964 192
13: Letters from the Field 196

Part Three

14: Homecoming. 217
15: S.M.U.. 221
16: Building Community 230
17: An Accident 244
18: New Horizons. 248
19: Bringing the World to Dallas 258

Part Four

20: A Journey in Faith. 277

Introduction

To have another language is to possess a second soul.
—CHARLEMAGNE 742–771

On December 6, 2010, as this book was going to press, Roy Richard Rubottom died peacefully in Austin, Texas. He was 98 years of age.

It can be argued that Ambassador Richard Rubottom's most important professional decision was made in 1926 when, as a high school student in Brownwood, Texas, he decided to take Spanish.

"It all started in that home-town classroom," Rubottom says today. "I was captivated by the Spanish language, and I really wanted to be able to converse, to read, and to write in Spanish. If I hadn't learned the language, I would have had an entirely different career."

As it was, Rubottom enjoyed two separate and highly successful professional lives, both informed by his understanding of the Spanish language and of the discrete parts of Latin America.

His first career began during World War II. Like so many young men of his generation, Dick wanted to do his part during the war, so he applied for a Naval Commission and eventually reported to the 8th Naval District Headquarters in New Orleans, where he was in charge of personnel and training of the District Intelligence Headquarters.

Because Dick spoke Spanish, he and his new bride, Billy Ruth, were sent to Manzanillo, Mexico, for Dick's first posting. He was next transferred to Asuncion, Paraguay, as Naval Attaché at the U.S. Embassy. While there, he decided to take the test for Foreign Service officers through the U.S. State Department. With that, his course was set. When he left the Navy, he entered the career foreign service by examination, rising in thirteen years to the position of Ambassador to Argentina, which rank would mark the apex of his diplomatic career.

However, Rubottom does not consider his time as an Ambassador his most significant contribution. He's matter-of-fact as he says, "Actually, I'd say the most important work I did as a Foreign Service Officer was when I was on the Mexican desk in the State Department, and I helped renegotiate the *Bracero* Agreement. Later I was promoted to Deputy Director of Middle American Affairs, and a while after that, I was named Assistant Secretary of State for Inter-American Affairs for the State Department. My responsibilities covered Mexico, Central America, the Caribbean, and South America.

"In those days," he goes on, "people weren't particularly interested in Latin America, so part of my job was to bring attention to those parts of the world, and to serve as a bridge between the United States and those cultures."

Rubottom retired from the State Department at the age of fifty-two and embarked on a second career, as Vice-President, teacher and lecturer at his alma mater, the university from which he earned Bachelor's and Master's degrees in Latin-American Studies in the early 1930s: Southern Methodist University (S.M.U.) in Dallas.

Even after retirement, Rubottom remained active in

diplomacy. At the age of 73, he became Director of the Office of International Affairs for the city of Dallas. Meanwhile, he was an advisor to Texas Governor Bill Clements and served on the Ethics Committee of the Texas Bar Association. He remained active in the Council on World Affairs, the Boy Scouts of America, Lambda Chi Alpha, and, most significantly for him and Billy Ruth, Highland Park United Methodist Church. Throughout Dick's career and the family's many moves, in fact, church had been a constant in their lives. Wherever they were, they contributed to their local church by teaching, hosting dinners, leading committees, serving as lay leaders, and through countless other avenues of service.

As an expert on U.S. policy toward Central and South America, Rubottom has given lectures, classes, and forum speeches on Latin-American affairs, in venues all around the United States as well as in Latin America and Europe. He has consulted with policy-makers as, through the decades, his interest in U.S.–Latin American issues continues unabated.

Because Dick Rubottom was at the table for so many historic conversations and policy meetings, his speeches comprise an historic record of mid-Twentieth Century U.S.–Latin-American relations. His lectures, speeches, and scholarly papers, as well as official photographs, articles and profiles about Mr. Rubottom, are available as an archive called the "R. Richard Rubottom papers" in the DeGolyer Library* at SMU in Dallas. The link to the abstract for this extensive archive is: http://www.lib.utexas.edu/taro/smu/00139/smu-00139.html.

Keeping him grounded through his association with such political figures as Dwight Eisenhower, Richard Nixon, General George Marshall, John Foster Dulles, Fidel Castro,

---

*The DeGolyer Library is the principal repository at SMU for special collections in the humanities, the history of business, and the history of science and technology.

Dr. Milton Eisenhower, and the leaders and diplomats of nations from Mexico to Argentina, are three passages that Dick Rubottom long ago committed to memory.

"I repeat three affirmations to myself every day," he says. "Several times a day, in fact, I repeat them in this order: the Lord's Prayer; Mary Baker Eddy's Scientific Statement of Being; and the Twenty-Third Psalm."

—JANIS WILLIAMS

Part One

The Lord's Prayer

Our Father, which art in heaven: hallowed be thy name. Thy kingdom come, Thy will be done on earth as it is in heaven. Give us this day our daily bread, and forgive us our trespasses as we forgive those who trespass against us. And lead us not into temptation, but deliver us from evil. For Thine is the Kingdom, and the Power, and the Glory forever. Amen.

CHAPTER 1

1912–1928

This story starts in the late 1800s, with the Reverend W. D. Watkins, Richard Rubottom's grandfather, a Baptist preacher from Mississippi. Reverend Watkins, like most pastors, couldn't count on his work with the church to provide enough money for him to feed and clothe his family. He needed a regular job for that, so when he was offered a position as Superintendent of Buildings and Grounds at the newly formed Howard Payne College in 1890, Rev. Watkins packed his family up and moved them to Brownwood, a small Central Texas city in the rolling hills of Brown County.

Howard Payne College was barely off the ground when Reverend Watkins, his wife, and their nine children arrived in town. The college had been founded at Indian Creek only the previous year, on June 20, 1889, by the Pecan Valley Baptist Association. The founders were two Baptist preachers. The brother-in-law of one of them, Edward Howard Payne of Missouri, gave a large monetary gift to the college, and later that same year the Board of Trustees voted to name the school after him. The college opened on September 16, 1890, with a faculty of twelve. Its first academic degree was granted in 1895.

So Reverend Watkins signed on as head of custodial

care. "My grandfather kept the place running," remembers Richard Rubottom. "At one time, when my mother was a girl, Howard Payne had a secondary school in addition to the college, so the grounds were large, and running the campus was not easy.

"So being a custodian was my grandfather's *main* job, though not his only one. On weekends, after working full time during the week, Grandfather went around to various little rural churches in the area to preach. He and my grandmother had a dozen mouths to feed, and somehow they did it. I remember my grandmother as a sweet, quiet woman, but she must have worked very, very hard."

Dick Rubottom's mother, Jennie Eleanor Watkins, was the second oldest of Reverend and Mrs. Watkins' nine children, having been born in 1880 in Mississippi. She was ten years old when the family moved to Texas, and after she graduated from Howard Payne Academy at age seventeen, she knew she was on her own financially. She certainly

Reverend William David Watkins and his wife, Martha Ann Hurst, were Rubottom's maternal grandparents.

wouldn't expect her father to keep supporting her now that she was out of school. She needed to find a job.

She decided to go to the booming south Texas city of Kingsville and begin training as a milliner. Once there, she became so good at her craft that the Ragland Department Store, where she worked, started using her as a buyer. She went as far as St. Louis to buy hats, and materials for hats—and she brought all kinds of fresh ideas back with her to Kingsville.

While she was working for Ragland's, Jennie met an imposing man of medium stature, with dark hair and eyes. His name was Roy Richard Rubottom, and he had been born in 1880 in Missouri. He worked at the Kleberg Bank when Jennie met him. The two young people fell in love and married there in Kingsville. Soon after, they moved to Wichita Falls.

Dick takes up the story. "It was in Wichita Falls that Mother became pregnant with me, but when her time came, she realized she wanted to be with her own mother when she gave birth to her first child. So she went home to Brownwood sometime during her ninth month.

Dick as an infant, held here by his mother, Jennie Eleanor Rubottom.

"My grandmother was a dorm mother at Howard Payne at that time, and of course my grandfather was still working as head of custodial staff. They looked after Mother until, and for a little while after, I was born in Brownwood on February 13, 1912."

When Mother and son

were both strong enough, they rejoined Dick's father in Wichita Falls, where he had a job at Security National Bank. In the months and years that followed, the little family continued to grow, with the first of Dick's younger sisters, Martha Frances, born in 1915, and his second sister, Nancy Merle, joining the family in 1917.

Asked whether he has memories from those years when the family lived together in Wichita Falls, Dick says, "I remember being given training in recognizing classical music. The school had a contest called the music memory contest. We grammar school students would listen to and identify classical music excerpts. I participated in this contest for two years, and that training constituted what little I knew about classical music before I began attending symphony concerts in Dallas many years later."

During the family's time in Wichita Falls, life was serene. But then came a turning point.

"It started when my father got a job selling banking equipment," Dick says. "This new job took us to Pittsburgh, Pennsylvania. Moving from a small city in the middle of Texas to a major city was an adjustment for the whole family. One big change was the weather. It was cold there! There was a downhill slope right in front of our house, and I used to sled there in the winter.

"Another big change, at least initially, was that Pittsburgh gave us our first experience with desegregated schools. All the public schools in the city were desegregated, so we had our first experience with African-American kids. That seemed natural to us, and it quickly became commonplace in our lives."

Dick and his parents and sisters lived in Pittsburgh for only two years, but in those two years, the children had several amazing opportunities. "For one, I was chosen to sing Christmas Carols with a children's choir on KDKA," he says. "That was the first radio broadcasting station in the

United States and it was right there in Pittsburgh. Experiences like that made me very aware of being in a major city, a modern city.

"Another advantage for me was that we lived near the Carnegie Museum. I remember going there in the summertime, when college kids would take us around and show us the paintings, and talk to us about the artists. You see, Carnegie Tech (now Carnegie Mellon) is famous for its Fine Arts program, so these students were enlisted to teach younger children about the arts. They functioned as mentors to us."

Rubottom notes a particularly happy memory that stands out for him. "My father arranged for me to take towels in to the Schenley Hotel in Pittsburgh. This is the hotel where visiting major league teams stayed when they played the Pittsburgh Pirates. As the hotel towel boy, I got to see the games free. That was very exciting."

This photo was taken in Pittsburgh in 1921, when the Rubottoms lived there during Dick's elementary school years.

Dick can't be sure, but he assumes his parents' marriage began to unravel during that period. "While we were in Pittsburgh, Dad was traveling a good bit of the time. I was the oldest child in the family, so it was pretty obvious to me that our parents' marriage had come under strain. I doubt if my sisters were aware of it, since they were so young. In any case, I don't remember my parents arguing. They didn't fight in front of us.

"But by the time I was twelve years old, they had drifted far apart. For one thing, since my father was on the road so much, Mother had all the responsibility for us children. She had no family nearby, and no old friends. She must have been lonely."

In any case, just before the beginning of the 1924–25 school year, Jennie Rubottom decided to move back to Texas with the children. "At first, my parents were only separated," recalls Dick. "When we got back to Brownwood, Mother rented a big house and started running it as a boarding house, working her fingers to the bone. We lived downstairs, and Mother had to cook and clean for anybody who stayed there. It was a hard life for her.

"Eventually my father divorced my mother and remarried," Dick says, "but before that happened, he visited Brownwood occasionally. He might have come twice while I was in high school.

"I don't want to be negative about my father, but after he and my mother divorced, he was not a vital part of my life."

Dick changes the subject by noting that moving back to Brownwood marked yet another adjustment for the Rubottom children. "At school, people were impressed that I had been in Pittsburgh schools and done well, so the powers that be moved me a grade ahead. This meant that I started high school at age twelve."

Was he bored to find himself in a small town after such a vital urban life? "No, no, there was no time for boredom. We had a Carnegie library in Brownwood, and in the summertime I read books by the dozens. I was very interested in the world. I loved reading about geography." From an early age, Rubottom worked every day after school. He did odd jobs, such as walking a little neighbor boy back and forth to school, and wringing chickens' necks for a grocer. He gave any pennies he earned to his mother, and tried to help by doing chores around the boarding house.

After his parents officially divorced, Dick gradually lost track of his father. "I don't think he ever supported my family," he says. "Financially, my mother was on her own."

Despite the struggles, though, the years of his life between age twelve and age sixteen were shaping ones for Rubottom. "The extended family gave me plenty of moral support at a time when I really needed it," he says. "My grandfather, for one, was a significant male figure to me. He was gruff, and not very confiding, but I appreciated the fact that he showed affection to me. He was a good man."

Dick remembers driving back to Mississippi with his grandparents one summer. "I rode in front, and my grandmother and another man sat in the back seat. My grandfather joked that Grandmother and that man were holding hands. It seems like every few miles we'd have a flat and I'd have to get out and change the tire. At some point during the trip, I came to the conclusion that one of the reasons Grandfather had invited me along was to fix flat tires. People had a lot of flats in those days."

Sometimes on weekends, Dick would accompany his grandfather on his church rounds. "I went with him, first by horse and buggy, later in a Ford Model-T, and still later in his Chevrolet car. He'd drive around to all these small country churches, and preach."

The extended family remained important to Dick and his sisters. "We had a number of cousins in Brownwood, and we spent lots of time together. We had fun. One female cousin, Leona Mckie, was closest to me, age-wise, so we went through the grades together, and later we were at

S.M.U. at the same time. Leona had studied piano all through her growing-up years, and she also studied voice under a well-known teacher at Howard Payne. At one point, I was invited to take a few voice lessons with her teacher, and that's where I learned how to harmonize.

"We were close to my Aunt Etha Lockwood and her husband and three kids: Maureen, Charles, and Harold. They were all kind to us. We often got together for Christmas dinner. Also, my uncle, Steve Mckie, liked to hunt and he'd shoot and bring home a wild turkey. For Thanksgiving, we'd make the traditional meal around that. Our holidays were usually spent at the Mckies' house.

"All in all, we had happy times with the extended family. Money was tight, yes, but these were the Depression years, and everybody was broke. We didn't really feel that different.

"I will say, though, that as soon as I graduated from S.M.U. and got a job, the first thing I did was to move Mother out of that boarding house and into a small apartment. I continued to support my mother for the rest of her life, as did my sisters."

In the spring of 1928, about a month before Dick's high school graduation, he got a surprise. "The principal invited me, along with three other boys—Calvin Bratton, Vernon Turner, and Billy Logan—to his office. 'I need you young fellows to calculate your respective grade-point averages,' he told us. 'We need to establish who has the highest academic average among the boys in your class.' He then handed us our four-year grade reports and it turned out that I won by .2. Our class valedictorian was a girl, and she was awarded a scholarship to Howard Payne, while I, by graduating with highest honors for boys, received a scholarship to Southern Methodist University in Dallas. I immediately decided to go there."

For his high school graduation, Dick's mother gave him

a little red Royal typewriter. "I carried it from then on," he says. "About halfway through the summer after graduation, I got a call from Howard Payne informing me that Mary Allison, the valedictorian, had turned down the Howard Payne scholarship. 'We are now happy to offer it to you,' the official said, and I replied, 'Well, you're about two months too late. I'm going to S.M.U.' And has that ever made a difference in my life!"

Dick graduated from high school at age 16, with the highest average among the boys in his class.

CHAPTER 2

1928–1938

At Southern Methodist University, Dick decided to major in journalism and minor in government, with an emphasis on Latin America—thus continuing his love affair with the Spanish language.

"Leaving Brownwood, I cut my ties pretty completely," he remembers, "except, of course, with my family. My life began to center around S.M.U., where I was very busy with campus activities. I liked sports, but I had limited time for them. I'd played tennis as a boy, and I made freshman letter in tennis at S.M.U. I guess I was decent at the game, but I had to give it up. I needed to work to pay my way through school."

To that end, Dick had a variety of jobs. "I worked at a movie theatre, four hours one day and eight hours the next. I was usher, ticket seller, ticket taker, popcorn seller—just whatever they needed. I was one of three or four students who worked under a manager named Paul Scott. With the money I earned, I was able to get by. However, I'm sure my grades suffered. I finished S.M.U. with a B+ average, but if I hadn't been working so much, I might have done better."

The first year he was in college, when he was seventeen years old, Dick's grandfather died. "I couldn't get home for the funeral," he says. "With my studies, my work schedule, and my lack of funds, it was impossible. But Grandfather was an important figure in my life, and I knew I would miss him."

The summer after freshman year, Dick needed a job. He had to earn the money for his next year in college. "That was the summer I worked on the Santa Fe railroad signal gang, all over West Texas and New Mexico. There were about nineteen men on the job that summer, and we all lived together in a converted railroad car that moved along with us. The foreman's wife would prepare our meals, and we'd each pay her for what we ate. I'll tell you, that was the hardest work I ever did in my life. In fact, I went to the foreman after the first day on the job and handed in my resignation. I told him, 'I don't think I can do this. I just don't think I can take a whole summer of it.' I told him I had decided to go on home and find another job. He said that was okay, but I'd have to pay my own transportation home. 'The company will pay to bring you out here to work,' he explained, 'but it's not going to pay to send you home.'

"Well, I thought it over for a day, then for another day, and by the time another few days had passed, I'd begun to adjust. But that was back-breaking work. A signal gang works with these signals that you see all along a railroad track. The lowest-rung members of the gang—me, in this case—were charged with shoveling gravel out from between the tracks so our co-workers could lay the electrical lines for the signals. Then, once the lines were laid, we had to shovel the gravel back into place—and we had to do all this in the west Texas heat. But the good thing was, I managed to save a hundred dollars that summer."

Lambda Chi Alpha, a social fraternity founded in 1909, was still relatively new when Dick was at

S.M.U. But when he was a sophomore, he met a few brothers, who took him to the Lambda Chi house, where he met others including All-American football player Logan Ford. The members invited him to pledge. Asked how that made him feel, Dick says, "I liked the guys, but I was broke. I had the $50 my mother had given me, plus whatever I could earn from my job. I didn't think I could afford to pledge."

He managed it, though, and once he had joined, he was elected pledge captain, treasurer, vice-president, and eventually president. This began his long and loyal association with the fraternity. Lambda Chi Alpha became a very important part of his life while he was at S.M.U.

In college at SMU from 1928–1933, Dick found membership in his fraternity, Lambda Chi Alpha, early preparation for a life of diplomacy and meeting the public.

Dick also served as Associate Editor of the campus newspaper, a job he enjoyed so much that, when he was a senior, he ran for editor. "I was elected editor, but I learned I would have to stay on campus an extra year in order to serve in the job, because a fraternity brother of mine was editor my senior year. I quickly made the decision to stay and do the editor's job. Then one day I ran into the Graduate Dean on campus and he asked, 'What are you going to do next year, besides editing the paper?' I said I thought I would take a few additional courses, perhaps in Latin-American studies. The Dean then invited me to visit him in his office, and when I did, he offered me the Arnold Fellowship in Government, which would pay my tuition for an M.A. degree. It was then that I decided to earn a Master's in Government, with an emphasis in Latin-American Studies. A Master's degree was rare at that time. It was comparable to today's Ph.D."

From the @Brownwood Bulletin, 1932

Roy R. Rubottom Is Awarded Arnold Fellowship at S.M.U.

Roy Richard Rubottom, son of Mrs. R.R. Rubottom of this city, has recently been awarded the Arnold Fellowship in Government at Southern Methodist University, according to word received here.

Young Rubottom will receive his B.S. degree in journalism at the university in June, and will be a candidate for M.A. in Government in June 1933.

He is also editor of the semi-weekly *Campus* for 1932-33, having served as sports editor and assistant editor of the university publication. He is also president of the fraternity Lambda Chi Alpha, for 1932, and is performing his duties as president and editor.

Dick's mother came to see her son receive his Master's degree.

It turned out the S.M.U. newspaper editor's job held clear advantages for a young man of twenty. "My family didn't have a car when I was growing up," Rubottom says, "but I bought a car when I was associate editor and editor of the campus newspaper, because I had to take all the copy down to the printer twice a week. The Arnold Fellowship in Government provided me $600 for the school year. In addition, the editor's job paid $500, which meant I had a guaranteed income of $1,100 for that year of study. It was the first year I'd ever been relieved of worry about how I was going to pay tuition and living expenses."

Rubottom took four graduate courses in government during that academic year. "As it turned out, it was very fortunate that I went ahead and earned my M.A. I was only twenty-one when I completed the work, and an M.A. in those years opened lots of doors."

When he left SMU in 1933, Dick had earned both a bachelor's and a master's degree.

Rubottom's roommate during these years was a young man named Willis Tate. Tate had been born in Denver, but he grew up in Dallas and San Antonio. With a major in sociology, he, like Rubottom, earned a Bachelor's degree in 1931 and a Master's in 1935. In addition, he was an honorable mention All-American football player in 1931. An enduring friendship grew between the two young men, and these early shared experiences forged a loyalty and mutual respect that would play a pivotal role in both their lives in the years to follow.

In the summer of 1933, Rubottom began writing his thesis, "The League of Nations and the Codification of International Law." "As it turned out, a few years later, in 1936, the League of Nations was dissolved," he says. "After World War II, it was replaced by the United Nations."

As soon as he completed his thesis and was awarded his M.A., Dick became Traveling Consultant, or secretary, of his fraternity, Lambda Chi Alpha. "This was a two-year assignment," he says, "and there were two of us dividing the work. During the first year, I traveled the western half of the United States, and during the second year, I traveled the eastern half. My job was to call on fraternity chapters in colleges throughout the U.S. I was also calling on Deans and Presidents of universities. Then I would write a report to send to headquarters in Indianapolis. The other traveling secretary and I got around mostly by train. I had sold my Model-A Ford for $90 after buying it for $100 and driving it for two years."

Although the Great Depression was in full swing at the time Dick earned his two degrees, he graduated owing only $500. "I owed that sum to the Miller family, my aunt and uncle by marriage who lived in Dallas. They had been very good to me while I was in S.M.U., inviting me over for Thanksgiving dinner, et cetera. Mr. Miller even loaned me $500 at one point. Then, when I got my degree and was hired for my first job, Mr. Miller reminded me that I owed him $500."

He chuckles. "I hadn't counted on having to pay him back. But of course I did pay him back. I felt really prosperous while I was traveling secretary. I was even able to send my mother fifty dollars a month."

Dick deeply admired his mother, and he says, "She was a remarkable woman, and very strong. When she was in her forties, she discovered the Christian Science faith through a small congregation there in Brownwood, and this sustained her. It helped her get through the pain of the divorce. Somehow it gave her a context for dealing with the hardships she had endured, and would endure. I've seen the evidence of what a spiritual foundation means to a person.

It can't have been easy to be a divorced mother of three children in those years, but Mother managed it beautifully. She was a great role model.

"As to my father, he remained a distant part of our lives for a few years, and then he disappeared. Actually, I met him only twice

Jennie Eleanor Rubottom, Dick's mother.

as an adult. Once, when I was at S.M.U., he came to visit me. I remember very little of that visit.

"The second time I saw him was years later, when I was in the State Department and Billy Ruth and the children and I were living in Washington, D.C. My father, who lived somewhere in Pennsylvania, came to Washington with his then-wife, and he telephoned me. I'd been mentioned in the paper a few times, and I'm sure he was curious about me, especially since we had the same name. Perhaps he even had some affection for me. In any case, we met at a hotel near Union Station. I took my family with me so that he could meet Billy Ruth and our first two children, Eleanor and Rick. John hadn't yet been born. I remember that visit as short and rather formal."

He concludes, in wry understatement, "My admiration for my father was limited."

After he finished his job with Lambda Chi, in the summer of 1935, Dick began to consider his long-term prospects. He was twenty-three years old, and it was time to get on with his career. "I gave it some thought and decided I'd like to be a Dean of Students," he says. "I liked university life, and I figured this would be a stable and productive career path. So I applied for the position of Assistant Dean under the well-known and highly respected V. I. Moore, then Dean of Students at the University of Texas in Austin. I wouldn't have been considered for the position if I hadn't had the M.A. in Government. Another thing in my favor was that I'd had the experience of calling on deans and presidents for the fraternity, and therefore I had an idea of what the work entailed.

"Even so, there wasn't a position for me. Dean Moore explained that he simply didn't have the funding to hire another person, but he also said that he would call me if he could locate the money.

"Well, I had to work. My best friend at the time was Page Colborn. His father owned an aluminum cookware company, and I let them talk me into becoming a door-to-door salesman of pots and pans. As such, I went to Chicago, and there I was, in winter, driving up and down those cold, snowy streets, knocking on doors and offering to cook meals for potential customers so I could show off the cookware. That was probably the second hardest job I ever had, after the railroad job.

"After a few months, I wanted to get back to Texas, to be near home and look after my mother. So I moved to Dallas and continued to sell cookware as I waited to hear from Dean Moore.

(l-r) Dick's mother, Jennie Eleanor Rubottom; his sister Nancy Merle; Dick; his sister Martha Frances

"The weeks passed, and I got tired of selling, so I went to work for the Guiberson Corporation, in the East Texas oil fields. I continued there for almost a year, living in Kilgore. They were selling oilfield equipment, and my job was to deliver packers and tubing catchers for the oil wells. Tubing catchers were parts that were installed in the drilling pipe so that, if anything happened and it broke, the catchers would expand and hold the pipe in place. I considered the work clean and honest, but it held no long-term promise for me. I was waiting to hear that a job had opened for me at U.T. I knew V .I. Moore was a man of integrity. I could tell he was impressed with me, and I understood that he needed help. He had only one assistant at the time. So I remained hopeful."

Finally, in the fall of 1937, when Dick was twenty-five years old, he did get the coveted call from Dean Moore. "Is this Roy Richard Rubottom?" came the voice from the other end of the line.

"Yes, sir."

"This is V. I. Moore. I told you I would hire you as soon as I got an appropriation to pay the salary. Well, I have that money now. Can you be here in thirty days?"

Excited, Dick replied, "Yes, sir. I'll be there."

How had the Dean even found Rubottom? "I later learned that he had called my good friend Zumbrunnen, who was Dean of Students at S.M.U., and from him Dean Moore had learned my whereabouts. This was a breakthrough in my life."

Within a week Dick had moved to Austin. "I thought it would be nice to be in the state capital, and I looked forward to being back in a university setting," he recalls. "Austin was a nice city then, with a population of about 90,000."

Dick's first day on the job was significant for more reasons than he might have predicted. "I met Billy Ruth the first day of work at my new job," he says. "The other assistant dean was a fellow named Shorty Nowotny. When Shorty invited me to have coffee with him about 9:00 that first morning, he said, 'There's a curly-headed brunette who works in the president's office. Why not invite her along?'"

Billy Ruth Young, about the time she met Dick Rubottom. 1937.

This, of course, was Billy Ruth Young, a co-ed from Corsicana with dark eyes and a beautiful complexion. Recalls Dick, "She went for coffee with us, and my first impression of her was very, very favorable. I asked her for a date on the spot. Soon, I learned that she liked to dance. I liked to dance, too, so we went to a little café out in Round Rock and danced the evening away."

As it happened, Billy Ruth had already heard of Dick. In a story that has subsequently made its way into the family lore, a few days earlier Billy Ruth had been helping the Dean file paperwork on incoming employees. When she read the name *Rubottom*, she made the comment, "I'm surely glad that isn't *my* name."

The Dean reminded her of this remark when, a year and a half later, she and Dick were married in a beautiful ceremony in the First Methodist Church in Corsicana. The date was December 23, 1938.

"Our wedding day was cold and rainy," Dick remembers, "but the wedding itself was happy. After the reception, we drove to Waco and stopped there for lunch. When I took my cap off, rice shook out from it onto the table. There were several students in the café, and they smiled and laughed, knowing we had just gotten married.

"After lunch, we made our way to San Antonio, where we enjoyed a three-day honeymoon at a historic downtown hotel."

On the Rubottoms' wedding day they posed with their mothers. (làr) Anna Eulalia Young, Billy Ruth Young Rubottom, Dick Rubottom, Jennie Eleanor Rubottom. December 23, 1938.

Chapter 3

1938–1946

After the honeymoon, the newlyweds returned to Austin and began their life together. Asked to recall those years, Rubottom says, "Well, because of nepotism laws, Billy Ruth had to resign from her position in the President's office after we were married. She got a job working at the N.Y.A., or National Youth Administration, which was prominent in those days. This was an organization that offered jobs and made loans to university students.

"Meanwhile, I learned a great deal from Dean Moore, and also from Shorty Nowatny. On a couple of occasions, Dean Moore invited Billy Ruth and me to accompany him and his wife to international meetings. Those were wonderful learning experiences.

"Billy Ruth and I lived in a small apartment about six or eight blocks north of the campus, just west of Guadalupe. Neither of us had any money when we married, and in addition we were in debt, with each of us owing $500 for our education. That was a considerable amount of money in the late 1930s, and we felt the burden of it. Therefore, the first thing we did was to pay off that debt, after which we began to save a little from our two working salaries.

"We had such fun as newlyweds. We would go dancing,

After a brief wedding trip, Dick carried Billy Ruth across the threshold of their first home. Austin, Texas, January 1939.

or go out to dinner or plays with friends. One of our favorite dance venues was the little place in Round Rock where we'd gone on our first date. They had a nickelodeon there."

Once embarked on the career of a college administrator, Dick found he enjoyed being back in an academic setting, and he also liked his colleagues at work.

After only one semester at his job, Dick began pursuing the Doctorate in Latin America Area Studies at the University of Texas in Austin, with the intention of majoring in Government. He says, "I took courses under two very distinguished people there: an historian named Charles Wilson Hackett, and a government professor named J. Lloyd Meacham." Four happy and productive years passed in this manner, as Dick accumulated forty or fifty graduate hours.

Then history intervened. World War II had begun to loom over the lives of all Americans. Like everyone, Dick and Billy Ruth gave events in Europe and Asia a great deal of thought.

"I was within the age group that was vulnerable to be drafted," Dick says, "and besides, I *wanted* to get involved. I wanted to be part of the war effort. The more we young men learned about what was going on in Europe, the more we wanted to step up.

"One day around that time, a tall, handsome Naval officer walked into my office wearing a crisp white uniform and spit-shined shoes. 'What's your uniform, and where in the world have you been?' I asked him, and he replied, 'I'm on active duty as a chaplain. I've been in the naval reserve.' I learned he was an Episcopal priest, and that he had been posted to a number of faraway places. At the end of our conversation, he asked me, 'Would you be interested in applying for a commission?'

"This seemed exactly right to me. I told him I would indeed be interested, so he sent me a form and I applied for a Commission in the fall of 1940. I received it seven months later, in mid-summer 1941, and that started my military career."

Rubottom was called into active duty in August 1941, just a few months before Pearl Harbor. "I was in the 8th Naval District Intelligence office in New Orleans," he says. "Billy Ruth and I moved to Louisiana, where I was in charge of personnel and training in the District Intelligence Office in New Orleans. It was wonderful being in that vital southern city. We were young, newly married, and we had no children. We both enjoyed music and dancing. Also, all of New Orleans, you might say, extended a very warm welcome to military visitors who came there early in World War II."

Dick jokes that when he got his commission and became a Lieutenant (JG) U.S.N.R., every friend he had ever had descended on him. "They all wanted to get into Naval Intelligence, especially after Pearl Harbor."

Dick joined the U.S. Navy and received his Navy Commission in 1941.

Billy Ruth Rubottom as a newlywed.

While the Rubottoms were still in New Orleans, Billy Ruth learned she was pregnant. About the same time, Dick found out he would be posted to Manzanillo, Mexico, for his next military assignment. It was decided that Billy Ruth would return to her family in Corsicana to have the baby.

"Her mother and father, aunts and uncles, sisters and brother all lived in the area around Corsicana," says Dick, "so Billy Ruth went home and our daughter, Eleanor Ann, was born in Texas on October 18, 1943. As soon as the baby and Billy Ruth were able to travel, they joined me in Manzanillo."

Manzanillo is north of Acapulco and south of Mazatlan, on the west coast of Mexico. Dick served as Naval Liaison Officer there for two years. "This was my first time to live in a Spanish-speaking country, where I could use my high school and university study of the language. Billy Ruth had never formally studied Spanish, but she learned the language through total immersion. There was only one other English-speaking female in the city, as far as we knew.

"In Manzanillo, all my previous study was put to use. We were at the service of small navy craft on their way to the war in the Pacific. We were the halfway point between the Panama Canal and San Diego, but we were not a U.S. Naval Base. Even so, ships stopped in Manzanillo to refuel, get water, and restock food supplies. My title was liaison officer, and I would coordinate with the Mexican navy. Except for one Chief Petty Officer, I had no staff. The Chief Petty Officer and I, and two yeomen who worked with us, coordinated all that traffic, just we and the Mexican navy. We had to keep contact with PEMEX, the Mexican Oil Company, to be sure there was always enough fuel, and to keep the water supply coming, which was difficult because the water came from a long distance.

"Many people don't even realize Mexico was in the war, but she fought on the Allied side. Admittedly, things were relatively quiet in Manzanillo, but I do recall that Mexico sent a squadron of airplanes out to the Philippines during the last phase of the war. Because the Mexican navy was comparatively small, it was not the most vital part of Mexican military. It was less important than the Mexican army and air force, for example. Still, it had its role to play."

In 1945, Dick was transferred to Asunción, Paraguay. He, Billy Ruth, and the infant Eleanor moved, and he took up his first assignment in South America. "I was doing what you might call intelligence work for the navy," he says, "reporting on what was happening in Paraguay. This was at the end of the war. Officially, I was on the American Embassy staff, with the title of Naval Attaché to the American Embassy. We also had an Army

When Rubottom was in the Navy, he was sent to Manzanillo, Mexico. Here with Billy Ruth at a restaurant in Manzanillo. This was likely a rotary luncheon, as Dick joined the Rotary wherever he was posted.

Attaché and an Air Corps Attaché, and all of us worked closely with the Paraguayan military."

Rubottom's duties were diplomatic. "We had a lot of parties—for which Billy Ruth was a marvelous hostess. The people in Paraguay speak Spanish and Guarani (gwar uh NEE), which is an Indian language that originated in the eastern part of Paraguay. When we lived there, every native Paraguayan spoke Guarani. Everybody was bi-lingual."

On October 19, 1945, the Rubottoms' second child, a son they named Frank Richard and called Rick, was born in Paraguay. The growing family stayed in Paraguay until after the war had ended.

In a Christmas newsletter written in December of 1945, Dick mused, "Being Naval attaché in the American Embassy in Paraguay is a lot different from our job in Mexico. It has been rather like moving from the country to the big city, and each life has its own advantages. Our 6,000-mile trip was a strange mixture. First, two weeks on an army transport with Billy and E.A. the only ladies on board, and all of us joining the 'order of the deep' when we crossed the Equator. Then two fast days of airplane riding brought us here on 4 July. We've encountered a surprisingly good climate, though in reverse. Bountiful foods of all kinds, and excellent servants. Asunción is modern in some respects, e.g. plenty of electricity; yet there is no running water (fortunately, we have a good well and pump). Oxcarts are still the stand-by of transportation and all but a few streets are cobblestone. Most everything but basic foods, wood, and leather must be imported; thus prices are high. Strikes and decreased production at home are immediately felt in countries like this."

"We didn't get back to the United States until 1946," Rubottom says. "Paraguay, like some parts of Argentina, had attracted thousands of German settlers, and part of my job was to keep an eye on them. The U.S. government remained interested in what Germans were doing all around the globe.

"I think every country in Latin America eventually joined the Allied effort. At first, there were two officers in my office: the naval attaché (me) and the assistant naval

During Dick's Naval service, the young family was posted to Paraguay. In Asuncion, Paraguay, he shows toddler Eleanor Ann how to ride her tricycle. 1945.

attaché. When the war was over in 1945, I conferred with the U.S. ambassador, Willard Beaulac, and asked to close down my office. The Department of Navy authorized me to downsize to one officer (me) and one enlisted man."

Dick and Billy Ruth have happy memories of their time in Paraguay. "It was a wonderful assignment," he says. "We were given a housing allowance, which enabled us to rent a comfortable, nice house in the local area. For every posting we had abroad, we had a nurse, cook, and housekeeper. And when, later, I got into upper level jobs, I had a chauffeur as well."

Says Billy Ruth, as she sits nearby, "We had a staff, which allowed me to focus on the children and our entertaining responsibilities."

Though the Rubottoms were sad to say goodbye to Paraguay, their leave-taking unexpectedly turned into a story of nail-biting adventure, providing yet another testament to the wisdom of Dick's having learned Spanish.

It was a June morning in 1946 when the family was scheduled to depart for the United States. As it happened, a group of Paraguayan army colonels had decided that they did not like President Higinio Morinigo's democratic policies for the country, and on midnight of the very day the Rubottoms were leaving, a revolution erupted. Its epicenter was at a cavalry garrison a mile from the Pan-American airport.

Shots were heard throughout the night, not diminishing until six in the morning. With the sunrise a tentative quiet descended, and the Rubottoms tied an American flag over the front of their car and headed for the airport. When they were stopped at road blocks, Dick conversed with the soldiers in Spanish, eventually persuading them to let the family pass.

They made it to the airport, where the Pan-American plane was signaled to stop and pick them up. Remembering that narrow escape, Rubottom says, "I have always enjoyed interesting jobs."

At the end of that year, Dick and Billy Ruth had to make an important decision. "Would I remain in the navy, or should I apply for a career in the Foreign Service? I had become interested in the Foreign Service through my association with Ambassador Beaulac. He encouraged me to apply for a position through the War Manpower Act, whereby the Foreign Service made a special offer to people who had at least a college degree and who spoke a foreign language. Through that act, the Foreign Service was authorized to admit 250 officers. I decided to go to Washington and take the test."

After he completed the exam, Dick and Billy Ruth and the children returned to Corsicana, Texas, Billy's home town, where Dick worked as a Vice-President at State National Bank while they waited for Dick's test scores.

"It wasn't an easy test, but I passed it, and I became one of the first ten people to be accepted and admitted, thus becoming an F.S.O., or Foreign Service Officer." As an afterthought, he adds, "Why we don't use the term 'American Diplomat,' I don't know."

By whatever name, Dick Rubottom had embarked on a new career, one that would take him into all parts of Latin America.

Part Two

The Lord's Prayer
Padre Nuestro

Padre nuestro que estás en los cielos, Santificado sea tu Nombre. Venga tu reino, Hágase tu voluntad En la tierra como en el cielo. Danos hoy el pan de este día, y perdona nuestras deudas, como nosotros perdonamos nuestros deudores. y no nos dejes caer en al tentacion, sino que líbranos del malo. Amen/Así sea.

CHAPTER 4

1946–1948

Leaving the Navy with the rank of Commander, Rubottom entered the Foreign Service as Second Secretary of the Embassy because he spoke a second language, had military experience, scored well on the qualifying exam, and had commensurate educational background. Even with all that going for him, though, his first assignment turned out to be challenging. He was sent to Bogotá, Colombia, at the end of World War II.

There are clear ranks in the U.S. Foreign Service, and new Foreign Service Officers, or FSOs, are always aware of them. "When I was starting out, most brand-new appointees came in as Class Eight foreign service officers," Dick explains. "That's the lowest rank. Then a person advances to Class Seven, Class Six, and on through Class One. The titles are First, Second, and Third Secretary of Embassy, Counselor of Embassy, and Ambassador, followed by Career Minister, then Career Ambassador. Most career ambassadors are not political appointees. Approximately sixty percent of American ambassadors are career people, and forty percent are political appointees. I was a career diplomat, and I might add that career diplomats usually get the tough posts."

This is the family passport photo, showing Frank Richard (Rick) and Eleanor Ann with Billy Ruth, taken just before the Rubottoms left for Colombia.

For Dick's first assignment, he and the family arrived in Bogotá in July 1947, following a long voyage via Grace Line freighter. Eleanor Ann would soon be four years old, and Ricky was coming up on two. "It was no small achievement to off-load our furniture in Buenaventura," Dick recalls, "but one week later we were settled in our Bogotá residence."

The family moved into a two-story house with a garage, in a middle-class neighborhood of Bogotá. It was located only three blocks from the U.S. Embassy residence. "Billy Ruth planted sweet peas and before we knew it, the vines had grown all the way to the roof of the house," Dick recalls. The Rubottoms were soon installed with a house staff of three, including a nanny, a maid, and a cook—all of whose salaries the family paid.

It is commonly assumed that diplomats are highly compensated, but that was not the case for the Rubottoms. They didn't come from family money, as many do, and they soon learned to economize even while entertaining people from all over the world. Billy Ruth scouted out bargains, and called on family members in Texas to shop sales and send needed items to her and the children.

One of her most faithful correspondents was her sister, Frances, to whom Billy wrote at the end of 1948:

Frances, I always will need lipsticks—and if you ever see any on sale, do buy two or three for me. I've been using Stae-on lately and it helps some, but I certainly do use a lot of lipsticks here. I'm not going to buy any more winter clothes—even on sale (!!)—because we never know how long we will be here, and I truly think we can look forward to being transferred before this year is out. I'm sick and tired of what [clothes] I have, but I must wear them out, because our next post might be a hot weather climate.

Frances, I can write direct to the stores and have some of these things mailed to me—so please don't let me impose on your time, but I'm always hoping you can save a little by shopping for me. Will any of the stores there have sales on children's shoes after Christmas? I want to send you the sizes just in case. I won't need the shoes for a couple of months or more, but I like to stay

Dick with Eleanor and Rick in Bogotá. 1948.

ahead and if you happen to find a sale, please buy me brown oxfords—for Eleanor Ann—size 11½ C and Ricky—size 9D—That size and on up—skipping about a size in between. The ones with the composition sole called Neolite or Avonite certainly wear a lot better than leather, but you may not find them. Eleanor Ann is going to need black patent in 11½ C, too.

We have been busy—as usual. Last week I had twelve ladies for luncheon and bridge and it all worked out so well. Most of the Colombians had had me in their homes with beautiful parties, so I was anxious to have this work out nicely. Hermencia, the cook, is really a jewel and she worked so hard. We had creamed chicken, rice, broccoli, hot rolls, fruit salad cold, with ice cream. It all tasted good to me. Dick's secretary, Mrs. Narden, is being transferred to Cairo and we are having a farewell cocktail party for her tomorrow night with mostly Embassy people. About 60 in all, so I'm a little concerned about food. One of my favorite dishes is Empanadas—little meat pies, served very hot. Hermencia makes wonderful pastry and her empanadas are something. I'm going to fill them with canned chili tomorrow night and I believe that will make them good. We are going to have potato chips with a cheese dip, tuna fish sandwiches, black olives, peanuts, egg and shrimp sandwiches—and I do hope it is enough. Most people have turkey and ham, but I just can't afford it. From now to Christmas there will be lots of parties.

During their early childhood years in Bogotá, Eleanor and Rick attended a British school with children from other countries, as well as Colombian children whose parents wanted them to learn English. It was an academically rigorous school, where the children wore uniforms.

They made friends with other diplomats' children, but also with children from around the world.

That first year in Bogotá, Rubottom found himself acting as a liaison between the Colombian government and American missionaries—at least those who hadn't been driven out by the instability in that country. "The missionaries had many problems," Rubottom recalls, "and I spent so much time dealing with them that I acquired the nickname of 'the ecclesiastical attaché.'"

Colombia seemed the ideal venue for Rubottom. He says, "In view of my military and language experience in Latin America, it was not surprising that this was my first assignment. The post was certainly a fulfillment of my hopes, because it came at a time and place of historic importance. You see, Bogotá was to host the 9th Inter-American Conference of American States, beginning at the end of March 1948. This had been planned for years, as a means of consolidating the efforts of Western Hemisphere diplomats for three-quarters of a century. It was hoped the conference would produce a Charter—to be called the Organization of American States—to which all of the American Republics would adhere. It would spell out a cooperating system of free democratic states in Latin America. Most important of all to the Latin-American states was the sacred principle of non-intervention, which the United States had accepted at Montevideo in 1933."

In a 1990 interview for the Foreign Affairs Oral History Program at Georgetown University in Washington, D.C., Rubottom reflected on his own role in these pivotal events. "I had been there for seven or eight months, and the Ambassador had assigned me the junior work to get ready for the conference," he says. "Of course, the Ambassador took care of the senior work on major policy issues himself.

I was quite junior. In fact, we had a delegation of forty to fifty people, and lo and behold, when the list came out, I found myself the very bottom man on the totem pole: Technical Secretary of the U.S. Delegation. Even so, I followed the conference day to day, hour by hour. I sat right behind Secretary of State George C. Marshall when he made his principal speech. Among the Latin Americans, everybody was hoping that he would announce a Marshall Plan

General George C. Marshall signed this photograph, "To Mr. and Mrs. Rubottom, with my thanks and warm regards." 1948.

for Latin America, as he had done for the European war-devastated countries at Harvard the previous June. Well, he did not do that. He announced an extra $500 million loan capacity for the Export-Import Bank. I watched people deflating like pricked balloons when he made that speech. Many times I've wished that he had said, 'We're going to have a Marshall Plan for Latin America. It's going to be a $500 million loan capacity.' We would have gotten all the Public Relations advantage of that, and we could have put the same amount of money into the Export-Import Bank for management purposes. But he chose not to do that, and this became my first experience of seeing the United States fail to live up to the aspirations of Latin America. It had happened many times before and, sadly, it has happened many times since."

Asked why the U.S. chose not to extend this help to Latin America, Rubottom says, "Well, for one thing, no Latin-American country had suffered an armed attack during World War II. There was nothing approaching the post-war situation that Europe was in, and indeed, in the case of Argentina—and, to a lesser extent, Uruguay, Paraguay, and Chile—you had countries that were openly sympathetic to the Axis cause. As a matter of fact, Argentina had to be forced by Russia in 1945, literally *forced*, to declare war on the Axis powers."

Rubottom says further that Latin America was in the economic hegemony of the United States. "The advocates of doing business through the private sector, rather than through government assistance, were particularly strong. Opponents of a 'Marshall Plan' for Latin America had the strongest positions in the economic bureau in the State Department, and certainly in the Treasury Department. Even today I'm not sure that Latin America deserved a Marshall Plan, but for PR purposes, I wish we had called it that."

As the lowest-ranking diplomat for the conference, Rubottom was doing leg work, making arrangements, and keeping in touch with the junior members of other delegations.

The delegations for this historic meeting had arrived in Bogotá on March 31, 1948, and the conference opened the next day. The U.S. Ambassador to Colombia was a 49-year-old career diplomat named Willard L. Beaulac, with whom Rubottom worked closely. Ambassador Beaulac had been in Paraguay as U.S. Ambassador from 1944–1947, so he and Rubottom were already acquainted. Over the course of his career, Mr. Beaulac served as U.S. Ambassador to Paraguay, Colombia, Cuba, Chile and Argentina, and, like Rubottom, he was well-versed in U.S.–Latin-American relations. Rubottom recalls that the U.S. delegation to that conference was extremely prestigious, and included (in addition to Secretary of State Marshall) such luminaries as Commerce Secretary Averell Harriman; former Ambassador to Argentina Norman Armour; Ambassador to Peru William Pawley; Ambassador John Dreier, Director of the Office of Regional American Affairs, who later would become U.S. Ambassador to the Organization of American States; and many others.

"Brigadier General Pat Carter, whom I had not known before, was executive assistant to General Marshall, and as soon as people began arriving, he and I started working together on every imaginable detail, both personal and official," Dick recalls. "It was up to us to assure that a smooth and productive meeting would take place."

Meanwhile, General Marshall expressed a desire to have dinner in the home of a typical Foreign Service Officer, and the Rubottoms were chosen to host him. The date was set for April 9, 1948.

"Our dining table had five leaves," Dick says, "so we could seat fourteen. With the Ambassador's permission, we invited the Foreign Minister and his wife; another Colombian couple; our own Ambassador and Mrs. Beaulac, of course; and six other senior members of the American delegation."

Billy Ruth, a gracious and adept hostess who was becoming accustomed to giving official teas and dinners, sometimes on short notice, began busily planning for this formal dinner in their home. But it was not to be.

Formal affairs were an everyday part of the Rubottoms' life in the diplomatic corps. Here, they attend a diplomatic affair in Bogotá.

Dick explains that the political climate in Bogotá in 1948 was very unstable. "For five years prior to this time, Colombia had been under the military dictatorship of General Rojas Pinilla. Pinilla was ousted, and what followed was a system of government that was rudderless.

"A couple of years before this meeting, a high-level civilian committee of leaders of both Colombian political parties, Liberal and Conservative, including a former President, visited Washington," Dick says, "and what came from that meeting was a system that empowered them to implement a plan called *Paridad*, by which the Liberal Party would rule for four years, followed by four years of Conservative Party Rule—with the pattern repeating for eight more years. It was believed that this plan would save democracy in Colombia. The Liberals had had the first turn. At the time of our meeting, the Conservatives were in power, under the leadership of President Mariano Ospina."

Such was the backdrop against which the 9th Inter-American Conference of American States began its meeting that year.

On April 9, the day before General Marshall and the others were to join the Rubottoms for dinner, Dick hurried home for lunch and a quick break from the intensity of negotiations at the Conference. He wanted to see Billy Ruth, and check on how the dinner preparations were coming along.

In Colombia at that time, the liberal leader Jorge Eliécer Gaitán was running for the presidency of Colombia for a second time. He had won his party's primaries and he enjoyed extensive support from the Colombian people.

Rubottom says, "As I rested on the couch at home around 1:30 that afternoon, my secretary, who was temporarily assigned to the American delegation office in the Capitol, telephoned me to report that Gaitán had just been assassinated as he was entering the street from his office, which was only a few blocks from our house. My secretary further reported that a mob had gathered on the street immediately, and had started pillaging and looting everything in sight. Within only minutes, the mob had stormed the Capitol building. My secretary, forced to flee the mob's outrage, jumped from the window to the street, and she broke her ankle."

Dick's secretary was evacuated to Panama, and she never returned to Colombia.

"I telephoned Ambassador Beaulac at his residence to inform him of this breaking news, then joined him five minutes later to drive to the Embassy Chancery, located only three blocks from the Capitol. It became clear that, within hours of Gaitán's assassination, the entire city had erupted into violence.

"Seeing the street mobs, we left the car and took a roundabout approach on foot, but machete-waving men forced us away from the chancery, diverting us to an apartment building where some of the American delegation were housed. There we encountered a miracle! We still had, and never lost, telephone contact with the Embassy, a large delegation office just across the street, and our homes as well. Apparently the rioters had thought of everything except cutting the telephone lines.

"By mid-afternoon, all the radio stations in the city had been forcibly taken over by spokespeople for the Liberal Party and other dissidents, especially the Communists. Listeners were urged to join the street mobs; instructions for using wire cutters to enter and rob local stores were broadcast. Looting began almost immediately. Sharp-shooters who had entered most of the taller downtown buildings were taking aim at anyone they spotted on the streets. The police, meanwhile, had either disappeared or joined the mobs, wiping out all security except by the military.

"Liberal Party leaders had entered the Presidential

palace, trying to persuade President Ospina, a member of the Conservative Party, to abdicate, which he refused to do. It is fortunate that his adversaries did not resort to force, perhaps because the Presidential Guard remained loyal.

"By late that afternoon, from the downtown apartment where the Ambassador and I had joined some members of the American delegation, we saw trucks loaded with corpses drive by, and the dead, as we later confirmed, were mostly innocent civilians. Sadly, an estimated 1,500 people—perhaps more—were killed in the rioting. Virtually all of them were civilians: men, women, and children. Destruction was wide-spread and indiscriminate. In short, downtown Bogotá became a no-man's land with mob rule, out of control."

As luck would have it, the residential section in North Bogotá, where the Embassy residence and the Rubottoms' house were located, was spared the worst violence. Dick recalls that Colombian President Ospina, fearing the worst, actually sent his eight-year-old son to the American Embassy residence for safety.

"The child, of course, became a potentially dangerous liability," Dick says, "but he was invited in for humanitarian reasons. At dusk, I went with the Ambassador to his residence, where I spent the night on a sofa, with a curved antique scimitar as my only weapon. The few Marine guards were all downtown at the Embassy office, where they successfully held off the mob that had tried to storm the building. They also kept open the street in front, which led to the main American Conference delegation office in an upstairs apartment of that building."

The diplomats were scattered throughout the city that day, but they were able to stay in touch by phone as the riots raged on the streets outside.

The next day was April 10. "At 7:00 the next morning, the Ambassador and I went to General Marshall's residence," Dick says. "There we joined General Marshall, his assistant, Pat Carter, and Secretary of Commerce Averell Harriman. We needed to assess the situation and figure out how to proceed. We soon had visitors: Mexican Ambassador Luis Quintanilla and his aide, Carlos Peon del Valle. The Mexicans had ascertained that, in light of the prevailing violence in Bogotá, the Cuban and Argentine delegations wanted to cancel or postpone the Conference and return home. However, General Marshall was adamant that the conference continue, as was the Mexican delegation.

"But how? The Colombian Foreign Minister, as host, was the Chairman of the Conference, but he was not really functioning, in light of the previous day's events. The Conference was bereft of leadership, and foundering."

Rubottom had an idea. "I knew a Colombian Senator well, a senior member of their delegation and Chairman of the Colombian Senate's Foreign Relations Committee. I agreed to try to reach him at home, to apprise him of whatever plans emerged. Meanwhile, the Honduran Foreign Minister was Vice-Chairman of the Conference. Remember, the Colombians were prostrate, almost out of business. As luck would have it, the residence to which the Honduran diplomat had been assigned had a large office beside the garage, large enough to hold a rump session of the remaining twenty Foreign Ministers. General Marshall and the Mexican delegate asked the Honduran to call an urgent meeting for that afternoon, April 10, at 3:00 p.m., and he agreed."

The next challenge facing the ministers was how to get the delegates there. "Because I knew the city, General Marshall made me the point man in this effort," Dick recalls. "I also knew the Colombians and most of the other delegates. I suggested that General Marshall assign me a jeep with driver and guard, flown in from Panama during the night. With that, I rounded up the downtown half of the delegates, where the sharpshooters were still busy.

"Meanwhile, my Mexican counterpart, Carlos Peon del Valle, gathered the delegations in the residential section of the city."

As Dick was about to depart on his assignment, General Marshall called him back. "Rubottom," he asked, "do you have an arm?"

Dick looked down at his bicep and said, "Yes, sir."

The General smiled. "No, I don't mean that kind." He called Pat Carter over and said, "Pat, go up to my room and bring me the box under my bed."

Pat returned with a box and handed it to General Marshall, who passed it over to Dick.

"I opened it," Dick recalls, "and found a Colt-45 pistol."

After Rubottom had notified everyone to come to the meeting, on the authority of the Secretary, he sought out the Chairman of the Senate Foreign Relations Committee of the Colombian Senate, whom he knew. He said, "I would like to inform you that we have decided to continue the conference. We realize that you may not be able to come, but we want to show you the courtesy of letting you know that we are going to do it and we do not intend to be run out of the city." Rubottom says that the Colombians appreciated being informed, and every delegation except for the Colombian attended the 3:00 p.m. meeting on that April 10.

"General Marshall spoke, as did the Mexican chair, saying that under no circumstances should the Conference fail to draft the Charter of the Organization of American States. He said further that to fail would play right into the hands of the Communists everywhere, who were taking credit for the attempt to destroy Bogotá. This forceful stand silenced the voices of the fearful and the uncertain, resulting in a unanimous vote to continue.

"Encouraged by that vote, the Colombians moved the Conference into a boys' school that was removed from downtown, and the sessions continued for twenty more days.

Negotiations were endless, but the delegates never lost sight of the goal: a Charter for the Organization of American States."

While Dick and the other officials were meeting to hammer out the Charter, Billy Ruth and the Rubottom children, along with two of the U.S. Ambassador's children, were isolated in the house, unable to leave, even to go into their yard to play. Billy Ruth stayed calm, thankful that she and Dick were able to communicate via telephone. She watched the children, directed the staff, and kept abreast of events in the streets outside as best she could.

After two days, she started a letter to her family. At the top of the sheet, she wrote: "Sunday night—52 hours after it started." Her letter supplies the back story of those historic events. It also provides a portent of her life to come as a diplomat's wife:

Dearest Family:

I'm sure you have heard the news broadcasts and I'm also sure you have worried—but please believe me that we are safe. The horrible catastrophe which has happened to Colombia is certainly true. The eye-witness reports of town are unbelievable. But you must remember that we are more than five miles from town, well locked into our house, and with police protection. We live in front of the Panamanian Embassy and they have four soldiers from the Army patrolling the front of their house.

We have more than enough food to last at least two weeks, so we have no need to send anyone outside. The government is beginning to get control enough that soon we will not have to worry. Our Army brought in a plane today from Panama with food, and many more will be coming. They are ready to evacuate everyone if neces- sary—but personally I want to sit tight because we are safe in our house and we can certainly care for our chil- dren better here. We also have the Beaulacs' two youngest with the nurse. The baby is nine months old now, and Nancy Ann is three and a half. The two older girls are staying with another friend.

You have all heard newscasts and read reports in the newspapers, but I'd like to tell you about our last two days, and fill in the rest from official reports. Friday 1:45 p.m., Mrs. Maebelle Narden, Dick's secretary, called from the Capitolio (where the Conference is being held) to say that there was a mob outside in the big plaza, and that she was locked in the offices of the U.S. delegation with two cleaning women, and what should she do??? Jorge Eliécer Gaitán had been shot a few min- utes after one o'clock and this was the first news we had received. It is difficult to put into the reports the true de- scription of Gaitán, because he was a man whom the Colombian people worshiped. He was almost a "god" to many of them and a truly powerful man. The reaction to his murder is sufficient testimony to his power—except I think that it started and then got out of control of every- one.

Anyway, when we got the news of his assassination, Dick told Mrs. Narden to sit tight, that help would be sent. But she finally jumped from a window, spraining her ankle. She was able to get back to the Embassy of- fice. Dick and the Ambassador started for the Embassy but were never able to reach it, so they worked most of the afternoon from a building on the outskirts of the busi- ness section, where most of the people in the U.S. dele- gation are housed.

The descriptions of the mob are really horrible. They

have completely destroyed all of the important public buildings and burned most of the churches (which action pointed to the Communists). Most of those churches were 300–400 years old. The entire business section has been sacked or burned. Army personnel who have been taking food to our people in the Embassy say that the first floors of all the buildings are empty. The mob apparently stole everything, including furniture and fixtures. The most serious problem now will be food for the people. Naturally we are concerned about all the delegations.

There has been no announcement yet about the Conference. I hardly see how they can continue to hold it here, but I hope they will make every effort, because I hate to give the Communists the satisfaction of breaking it up.

I have hardly seen Dick these last two days—but I know he is safe because he is working most of the time in the Embassy residence. He is certainly needed. He calls regularly, and of course Mrs. Beaulac and I keep in close touch. She is practically running a hotel at the Embassy Residence. Meanwhile, General Marshall is safe, with a lot of protection.

By the way, arrangements are being worked out to fly food in from Panama.

You can imagine how tired I am of being cooped up at home when the children are desperate to go outside and play. I'll write again soon and report in on any new developments.

Billy Ruth missed her family back in Corsicana perhaps even more than usual in those tense days. She wrote long, colorful letters to them, in which she detailed her life with Dick, described the children as they passed through infancy and toddlerhood, and discussed the world events in the middle of which she found herself.

Two days after she started the above letter, she added:

Even without seeing the middle of town I feel that it will take this country hundreds of years to recover from this revolution. Many have been killed and the economic problems ahead of them are tremendous. Last night Dick told me he talked with several of his friends in the government here and they are so dazed.

Meanwhile, as the delegation worked in its secret location in Bogotá, the biggest sticking point in negotiating the Charter, not surprisingly, was the economic section. The American position emphasized the free market and a private enterprise system, whereas the Latin-Americans supported a more centralized system with a strong government role, according to Rubottom. "Eventually, after four days of debate on that issue alone, a compromise was reached," he says.

Back home in Texas, the Young and Rubottom families were anxious about their kin. The following article appeared in the *Corsicana Daily Sun* on April 10, 1948.

Corsicanans in Bogotá

Several Corsicanans are in Bogotá, where revolutionary violence is raging.

No direct word from them had been received today, but the Associated Press listed only one American (not a Corsicanan) as injured.

R. R. Rubottom, Jr., former Corsicana banker, is the second secretary to the ambassador at Bogotá, and he is one of the three secretaries attached to the American delegation at the Inter-American conference. He was appointed to the consular service by President Truman in March 1947, and went to his present post in July.

Family in Bogotá

He resigned as Vice-President of the State National Bank here to enter the consular service. His family is with him. Mrs. Rubottom is the former Billy Ruth Young of Corsicana. Their daughter, Eleanor Ann, is 4½ years of age, and their son, Richard, is 2½ years old. Mr. and Mrs. Frank R. Young of Corsicana, parents of Mrs. Rubottom, had not received any word from the Rubottoms Saturday.

Frank Wright, 1946 graduate of Texas A&M College, is an engineer with the Texas company and resides in the Rubottom home. Wright is the son of Mr. and Mrs. B. F. Wright, 2111 West Second Avenue.

He has been in Bogotá a year and is planning to return home on a five-week' vacation, beginning April 29. His mother said he had already purchased his plane ticket for the vacation trip home.

Rubottom holds B.S. and M.A. degrees from SMU and finished his resident graduate work in Latin-American relations at the University of Texas prior to entering the U.S. Navy during the war. He was naval liaison officer in Manzanillo, Mexico, 1943-45, and naval attaché at the embassy in Asuncion, Paraguay, 1945-46.

Rubottom, an interesting speaker, frequently appeared on programs before local clubs and discussed political and economic life of Latin-American nations. He is a strong advocate of better understanding and closer relations with the Southern republics.

On April 15, Billy Ruth updated her family in a letter:

You know by now that all the fires are out and the Government is in control. There is still firing in the streets, because they can't seem to clean out all the snipers. Therefore, everyone stays pretty close to the house. We have had practically no disturbance in this section, but we stay home anyway. There is a 7:00 p.m. curfew and the streets are completely cleared by then.

Our army is flying planes in and evacuating those people who feel they must leave. A good friend of ours left yesterday for Panama. She's expecting her baby in about two weeks and they were afraid she might need a doctor at night and wouldn't be able to get help. A good part of our Embassy staff is staying at the building in town—they say they are getting pretty tired of eating rations from cans, so I'm making three pies to take down in the morning.

Dick has worked so hard—and he's doing a good job. General Marshall has given him some work to do and seems to value his opinion on local matters. The Conference is now meeting in a school about two blocks from our house. They have about 400 soldiers in this section to guard the Conference. A group of women is now working on the problem of feeding the soldiers. The Red Cross is also busy trying to help the wounded.

After many days in the house without mail or contact, Billy Ruth was reaching across the miles to her family, as she concluded her letter home:

I've knitted almost half a sock and will probably finish many before we get this thing settled. Since the post office was burned, we won't receive any letters written in the last couple of weeks. I don't even know how we'll mail this one. Maybe I'll try to send it to Panama on a U.S. plane. It will probably take a while to get things straightened out so they can handle the mail again—but please write soon. Do.

Love, Billy

As it turned out, of course, General Marshall did not dine with the Rubottoms. "I never saw him again," Dick says, "but I will always be grateful for having known and worked with him. Later in my career, the Organization of American States (OAS), with its Charter of Timeless Principles, was one of the most vital instruments for the conduct of U.S. foreign policy in the Americas. I was honored to have had a role in that."

Sadly, following Gaitán's assassination, Colombia descended into violence. Known throughout Latin America as *La Violencia*, the campaign of repression that overtook the country lasted for ten years and set the stage for further instability in the region.

As an epilogue to these historic events, Rubottom adds, "Important as it was and still is, the Charter of the Organization of American States is not always applied evenhandedly. One might say that there is a double standard. In 1960, for example, when the Trujillo dictatorship of the Dominican Republic attempted to intervene in Venezuela, it was easy to get and enforce sanctions against Trujillo, but the OAS would not sanction the Castro government in Cuba when it was blatantly intervening against its neighbor."

Dick deeply respected Secretary of State George Marshall for his courage during those events in Bogotá. He says, "When many delegates wanted to cancel the conference and go home, Marshall simply put his foot down. 'We're going to stay here and finish our work,' he said. I respected the way he kept that meeting going, because we had important work to do. Prior to this time, the only agreement among these countries had been the Pan-American Union, which didn't have any real power.

"History was made when the O.A.S. was formed, and

the organization subsequently became an important addition to U.S. diplomacy. If everybody had gone home when the city was overtaken by violence, who knows what would have happened in U.S.–Latin-American relations?"

The Rubottoms' Christmas card, 1949.

CHAPTER 5

1950–1951

In January 1950, after two and a half years in Bogotá, Dick was named Deputy Director of Mexican Affairs for the State Department. The Rubottoms returned to Washington, D.C., for this new assignment. Dick looked forward to the work. He was comfortable with Spanish and glad he could write in both languages. "I could compose short, directly to-the-point letters," he says. "On the Mexican desk, you spend considerable time either writing, or supervising the writing of, answers to hundreds of letters to Congress. Senators and Congressmen send over letters they receive and ask you to draft a reply."

Rubottom says at that time the Chamizal question was hovering in the background. Chamizal was a dispute over the riparian boundaries of the Rio Grande River, a feud that had started in the 19th century. Rubottom explains that "the difference of opinion arose over whether there was a sudden change in the river boundary, or whether it was gradual. Under international law, if a change is gradual, the boundary stays with the river. But if change is sudden, the boundary remains in place. For decades, nothing was done to settle this dispute, and then in the early 1900s, it erupted. When it reached the boiling point, the Americans and Mexicans called in the Canadians to mediate.

"Well, the Canadians listened to both sides and decided that Mexico was in the right, which meant that the boundary was awarded to Mexico. The result was that some of the United States' occupied land was now in Mexican territory. The U.S. refused to accept the decision, so the problem continued to simmer. It wasn't settled until 1963-64, when Lyndon Johnson was president."

Rubottom believes the issue could have been resolved ten years earlier. "When I was on the Mexican desk, in 1952-53, Deputy Assistant Secretary Tom Mann came to my office one day and said he wanted to discuss something with me. We went into the office and closed the door. For the next hour or so we studied a big map of the area and we saw how certain territory could be exchanged that would satisfy both sides. We agreed it was worth trying, so we called in the Minister Counselor of the Mexican Embassy and went over our thoughts with him. He wasn't too offended, and in fact he thought our idea might have merit. But he never came back with any answer. That's when we realized that in fact the Mexicans had found it convenient, up until that time, to keep the issue alive. They could bring it up any time they wanted, and apply leverage on disputes between the two countries. Then, finally, in 1963-64, they had wrung all the advantages they could out of it, so they decided it was time to settle. The Chamizal was settled then."

In her graceful way, Billy Ruth was adjusting to Washington: a new city, a new home, and a new set of activities for Eleanor Ann and Ricky. As was their habit, she and Dick started looking for a church home as soon as they arrived.

In a letter to her mother, written June 2, 1950, Billy Ruth described the experience.

We are truly enjoying Washington. Our only complaint is the high cost—but I guess that is true everywhere. I still feel fortunate in our apartment. We are hoping it will not be too hot this summer. We joined the Chevy Chase Methodist Church, and we go to the 9:30 service while the children are in Sunday School. We have been asked to organize a young adult group—age 23 to 35—and plan to start on it soon. The church doesn't have many activities through the summer, but we will try to get the group ready to start in September. The church has over 900 members and is really an active group of people. Something is happening all the time there, but of course we don't have time to join in everything.

Throughout 1950, Rubottom was engaged in a pivotal effort at work, a process he considered of paramount importance in U.S.–Mexican relations, as well as a high point in his own career: he was overseeing the re-negotiation of the *Bracero* Agreement between the United States and Mexico.

An enduring challenge in U.S.–Latin American relations has always been how to deal with workers from Mexico and Central America who come to the United States for jobs in agriculture. Throughout the 20th Century, U.S. and Mexican government officials addressed the fact that Mexican laborers are needed for agricultural labor in the U.S., yet a perfect—and permanent—solution to their illegal entry remained elusive.

This was never a simple matter. Back in 1942, on July 23rd that year, a bilateral agreement called the *Bracero* Agreement had been formalized. Through this agreement, Mexican agricultural workers were able to enter the United States legally to work. The word *bracero* is derived from the Spanish word *brazo*, meaning "arm," so used because these were manual laborers. Over time, the word *bracero* came to refer to the Mexican farm workers themselves.

During the years of America's involvement in World War II, 1942-1947, relatively few migrant workers were admitted to the U.S., but those who came were paid as much as U.S. workers doing similar work, or $0.30 an hour, whichever was higher. This was a guaranteed wage.

The first renegotiation of the *Bracero* Agreement took place on April 26, 1943, and it was titled "For the Temporary Migration of Mexican Agricultural Workers to the United States as Revised on April 26, 1943, by an Exchange of Notes between the American Embassy at Mexico City and the Mexican Ministry for Foreign Affairs." Following are the general provisions:

1) It is understood that Mexicans contracting to work in the United States shall not be engaged in any military service.
2) Mexicans entering the United States as the result of this understanding shall not suffer discriminatory acts of any kind in accordance with the Executive Order No. 8802 issued at the White House on June 25, 1941.
3) Mexicans entering the United States under this understanding shall enjoy the guarantees of transportation, living expenses and repatriation established in Article 29 of the Mexican Federal Labor Law . . .

The provisions then laid out, in exhaustive detail, issues of discrimination, pay, transportation, and, of course, duration of stay in the United States.

Because of the complexity of the issue, U.S. and Mexican officials returned to the negotiating table in 1949 and again in 1951 when, as Director of Mexican Affairs for the State Department, Dick found himself responsible for representing the U.S. position.

"This was the biggest negotiation between the United

States and Mexico at that time, and I worked on it for almost a year before we even got *to* the table," he says. "I was collaborating with my Mexican counterparts regularly, because we in the U.S. delegation didn't want simply to present the Mexicans with a finished product. We wanted their input and ideas. It was a matter of showing respect for the Mexican position."

In the early 1940s, Mexican workers had accounted for only about ten percent of agricultural workers in the U.S.,

A dressy evening in Washington, 1951.

and these were concentrated mainly in California and Texas. Yet as time passed, the U.S. agricultural industry became increasingly dependent on Mexican workers for harvesting crops and keeping the food supply moving.

The *Bracero* Agreement attempted to find a way for thousands of Mexicans to work legally in the United States agricultural industry, while also providing them the opportunity to go home at the end of the harvest season.

"I had two strong pressures as I considered the negotiations," Dick says. "The first came from the AFL-CIO, and the second from growers. The growers used Mexican labor, especially in California. They relied on this cheap labor. On the other side were the labor unions, who were concerned that the *braceros* were taking work from American laborers. Both groups were highly interested in our negotiations, and I took their concerns with me to the table."

As the talks continued over a period of months, Rubottom shuttled between Washington and Mexico City. "Toward the end of those negotiations, I was in the hotel in Mexico City, and there was a group of California growers in one nearby room, and a group of AFL-CIO representatives in another. Their concerns were not the same. Not at all. Each had fundamental items that they insisted should be included in the agreement. I would characterize their positions as self-serving and tough, but not unreasonable. The growers were already dependent on Mexican labor, while the AFL-CIO was concerned with fairness for U.S. workers. The two main issues were pay, and the ability to cross back and forth between the two countries.

"I started dealing with this conundrum as soon as I took the job of Director of Mexican Affairs, and negotiations went on and on, stretching from weeks into months.

"The problem of illegal Mexican farm workers in the U.S. had become critical. It was always my opinion that we should negotiate an agreement with Mexico, permitting her farm labor to enter the U.S. legally during the harvest season, then to return home, which most of them wanted to do anyway. Their dollar remittances to their families have long been a substantial source of Mexico's foreign exchange. However, the AFL-CIO continued to oppose such a plan."

According to the Congressional report, growers wanted "an orderly system for admitting Mexican workers that would guarantee the American producer an opportunity to harvest his crops and place them on the market for the good of all American Consumers." (U.S. Congress 1951, 6)

Also during those talks, Mexican representatives wanted to require the United States to impose sanctions on employers of illegal Mexican workers. The final agreement, however, did not include such sanctions.

Eventually the various sides did come to agreement, and the *Bracero* Agreement, as renegotiated under Rubottom's leadership, was approved in July 1951 and signed into law by President Harry Truman.

The version of the *Bracero* Agreement that Rubottom oversaw stayed in place from 1951 to 1968, when President Lyndon B. Johnson, under increasing pressure from the AFL-CIO, let it expire. "There ensued more than two decades without a legal basis for Mexican farm workers to enter the U.S.," says Rubottom. "After the hearings of the Hesburgh Commission* in the 1980s, some order was restored, but the basic problem remains even today. The need

---

*In 1981, the Rev. Theodore Hesburgh, then president of Notre Dame University, chaired a congressional commission to study immigration policy. In its report to President Ronald Reagan, the commission estimated U.S. population at 200,000,000, declaring that this number was "already ecologically unsustainable." The commission recommended an immediate freeze on immigration.

Hesburgh and other commission members highlighted the issue of "chain immigration," illustrating their findings with the example of a family of five immigrants. If all five members of this family became naturalized citizens, their number would grow in only a few years to reach eighty-four.

In 2010, just prior to the 2010 census, the U.S. population is estimated at 308,867,537; it continues to grow.

for labor exists. The labor supply exists. It is a push-pull geographic and economic reality that cannot be ignored without cost, even though the political reality is challenging."

The 1951 *Bracero* Agreement was more detailed than the 1942 agreement had been, and it included some complicated expectations. For example, the United States was to give Mexico at least thirty days' notice of how many workers would be needed, and then U.S. Department of Labor representatives were charged with interviewing workers at recruitment centers in the interior of Mexico, to determine who was qualified for farm work in the U.S. Selected *braceros* were transported to a reception center along the border, where contracting with the growers would begin.

In spite of the political, economic and human challenges that these issues presented, Rubottom remained optimistic about the relationship between the two neighbors. "Mexico and the United States are proud nations facing each other across two thousand miles of common frontier," he observes. "They share desert in the far west and the precious water of the Rio Grande for eight hundred miles in the eastern sector. They had the good sense and foresight to establish the Joint U.S.–Mexican Boundary and Water Commission more than a hundred years ago. The Commission headquarters are in Ciudad Juarez–El Paso, but branch offices have been established across the entire border. Their work is practical and technical, with virtually no sensitive political overtones. So it *can* be done."

CHAPTER 6

1951–1952

The *Bracero* negotiations constituted a high point in Rubottom's career, but his far-reaching influence in U.S.–Latin-American relations was just beginning. The following year, as Deputy Director of Middle American Affairs, which position included oversight of Mexico, Central America, and all the Caribbean, and which position he held for a year and a half, Rubottom was given the assignment of heading up the six-person team charged with negotiating a new trade agreement between the United States and Venezuela, to replace the trade agreement that had been reached between the two countries in 1939. This work took place both in Caracas and in Washington, D.C., which meant that for months Dick and his colleagues shuttled between the two cities.

With travel so much a part of Dick's work, Billy Ruth had to be in charge of the home and children, sometimes for days or even weeks at a time. "She was a wonderful mother," Dick says. "I have often said that the State Department got two employees for the salary of one when they hired me. Not only was Billy Ruth a marvelous hostess, but also she managed our household with calm and grace, and she took wonderful care of our children. The children, fortunately, were very adaptable. They did well wherever we went."

In Washington, the family settled in Silver Spring, Maryland, a close-in neighborhood. Dick and Billy Ruth became close friends with a group of neighbors from their block. These were not State Department employees, and, despite Dick's travel schedule, the Rubottoms enjoyed an idyllic family life during these years. There were no fences on the entire block, and the children could play outdoors for hours.

Billy continued to share the details of the family's life through letters home. On September 12, 1950, she wrote her parents,

Ricky had his first day in kindergarten today—it is hard for me to realize he will be five next month. Eleanor Ann is in the second grade and seems to like her teacher very much. They both will ride the bus, even though we live close to the school. The county has not cut the roads through, so the children in kindergarten, first and second grades will be taken by bus until the road is finished. I'm so glad, because by that time I'll feel safer about Ricky walking. They are calling him Frank in school and he says he likes it.

Dick and Billy Ruth had countless evening engagements during those years. "It was understood that entertaining would be a part of the job," Dick recalls. "But we managed to spend time with the children, and enjoy evening meals together. Also, we attended a local Methodist church regularly. Billy Ruth and I tried to make our home life as normal as possible for the children."

While Billy Ruth and the children settled into their routine in the nation's capital, Dick continued to make trip after trip to Venezuela as head of the negotiating team.

On at least two occasions, Billy Ruth accompanied him. When she did, Dick's mother or one of Billy Ruth's aunts would come to Washington to stay with the children.

"We were dealing with everything involving trade between the two countries," he recalls. "It was fascinating work. We were charged with setting the figures right on tariffs, among other things, and that alone took about six months. In a trade agreement negotiation, people from the State Department and the Department of Commerce are involved. Sometimes the Department of Labor is also brought in. As I recall, one member from the Embassy in Caracas was a friend of mine named Ray Leddy, and he, too, sat in on negotiations from time to time.

"As I have said before, there are many points of view in a negotiation, and many groups have an interest in what takes place. They all need to be welcomed to the table, and they all need to be listened to. Our team's role, of course, was to negotiate on behalf of all the interests of the United States, while our counterparts were negotiating on behalf of the various interests of Venezuela.

"The ultimate test of a diplomat is his or her ability to negotiate. When a diplomat sits down with the representatives of another country, he or she is representing the United States, and the people across the table are representing their own country. The charge is to find middle ground."

Clearly the stakes were high in the 1950s. At that time, sales of oil concessions in Venezuela brought more than $500 million in to the Venezuelan government, and most of that money was slated to be used for an enlarged public works program.

In a speech titled "Economic Prospects in Latin America" that Rubottom delivered before the Detroit Council of Foreign Relations in 1957, he recalled those negotiations. "A geographic breakdown shows that Venezuela contains the largest amount of our direct private invest-

ment, with $1.4 billion, almost all in the petroleum indus-
try. In addition, iron exports are increasing rapidly as a result of new finds, and American steel companies in the future will need to meet more of their ore requirements from
the new rich fields in Venezuela, Peru and Brazil."

While Rubottom was heading up these talks, oil production in Venezuela reached its highest level in history and
prices also increased. But he kept negotiating until
President Harry S. Truman sent a letter to the Congress of
the United States, which began:

> "On August 28, 1952, the United States signed an agree-
> ment with Venezuela which amends and supplements the
> Trade Agreement of 1939 between the two countries."

Thus the negotiations were successful as once again
Richard Rubottom used his skills to bridge borders, lan-
guage, and special interests to reach accord. For his efforts,
he was awarded the Superior Service Award in the State
Department, which high award was presented by Under-
Secretary of State David Kirkpatrick Este Bruce in 1952.

In recalling those heady days, Dick remarks, "Whatever
progress I made in the State Department was due to three
important negotiations: the *Bracero*, the U.S.–Venezuela
Trade Agreement, and a lend-lease agreement with Mexico
that I headed up."

These three negotiations established Rubottom as an able
negotiator, and he says, "Much of the negotiation, especially
in Mexico and South America, took place in Spanish. Since
not all members of the team spoke Spanish, my language
skills allowed me to translate when necessary."

Asked about that third negotiation, Rubottom explains
that the 1948 Lend-Lease Agreement with Mexico involved
several U.S. planes that Mexico had procured during World
War II. "The United States needed and wanted to be reim-
bursed for this expensive equipment. Mexico, for its part,

did not feel obligated to pay. My job was to persuade them that they were indeed obligated." Ultimately, under Dick's leadership, the two sides did come to agreement.

Within the State Department, Dick's reputation only grew.

At home, meantime, the Rubottom family grew. On October 5, 1952, Dick and Billy Ruth's third child, a son, was born. They named him John William Rubottom.

Merry Christmas
Happy New Year

**John William, born Oct. 5,
brings the Rubottom greetings**

In 1952, John William Rubottom was born in Washington, D.C.

Dearest Mother: Sunday

It was wonderful seeing you in Dallas. As usual, you were smartly groomed and looked wonderful. The whole family was interested in your activities and I so wish they could have joined me. Johnny weighed 13 lbs. today. Rocky and E. A. are going to the S. S. party later this afternoon. We are so busy with our material preparations for Christmas that I wish we could slow down a little for spiritual meditation. We all need to, don't you agree.

There has been no further development concerning Caracas, so the matter will probably be shelved for the time being.

We love you and send heartiest Christmas greetings. Always, Dick, Billy, & Tom

Rubottom maintained a lifetime correspondence with his mother. This is his note on the back of the family Christmas card in 1952.

CHAPTER 7

1953–1956

Because of his continued success as a negotiator, Dick was promoted, in 1953, to First Secretary of Embassy and sent to Spain. Once again he and Billy Ruth packed their bags, their furniture, and the children, and the family moved to Madrid.

In the book titled *Spain and the United States Since World War II*, co-written by Rubottom and J. Carter Murphy and published in 1984 by Praeger Publishers, Dick wrote, "Destiny drew Spain and the United States together."

He recalls, "The United States had only recently renewed our relationship with Spain. Because the country was still under the rule of Generalissimo Francisco Franco, many U.S. friends criticized us for this association. There was tremendous anti-Franco sentiment among our allies, owing to the fact of Franco's long dictatorship, and his having sided with the Axis during World War II. The British didn't like Franco. The French didn't like him."

Franco had been elected Commander-in-Chief of the Spanish Nationalists in September 1936, but after the death of General Emilio Mola, Franco became Spain's head of state. The party he headed, the *Falange Espanola Tradicionalista y de las Juntas de Ofensiva Nacional-*

Sindicalista, became the only party in Spain, which meant that Franco ruled with near absolute power.

After World War II broke out in Europe, in September 1939, Spain adopted a pro-Axis non-belligerent position. Although Spain offered, for example, Spanish naval facilities to German ships, Franco was opposed to Spain's entering the war. He met with Adolf Hitler in late 1940, but no agreement was reached and Spain remained outside the war—even if not precisely neutral.

As it turned out, Dick served as First Secretary of Embassy for only six months before he was again promoted, this time to Director of U.S. Operations Mission in Spain.

"The USOM job was an important one, dealing with economic as well as security issues," he says. In this position, Dick had an opportunity to put into practice some of his most strongly held principles of negotiation.

"In Spain, I observed at first hand the government headed by Generalissimo Franco," Dick says, "and I had to conduct one difficult economic negotiation after another with Franco's representatives. While not condoning the less attractive facets of the government by which Franco ruled Spain for twenty-five years, I slowly discerned the strength of character of the Spanish people as I talked to those who had suffered under the worst Civil War since our own. Above all I witnessed the establishment of a security partnership between Spain and the United States that served the interests of both countries, and indeed, the entire free world."

He goes on, "It's always important to consider the measures that we take to achieve our objectives, because foreign policy has no meaning at all if we don't have a line of initiative to be carried out by our people in the field, as well as those at home in the U.S. I believe in the aggressive execution of foreign policy. It seems to me that if a negotiator just waits until the problem has arisen and then tries to focus his attention on it and come up with a solution, he's not half as effective as if he applied the same amount of brain power in advance. It's critical that a negotiator set objectives, and try to guide opinion, guide governments, etc., in the best way that he can, through whatever powers of persuasion and other pressures that he can bring to bear. Only then can he achieve the stated objectives, and perhaps avoid problems."

As regards Spain at that time, and the rule of Franco, Rubottom adds, "Experience has demonstrated repeatedly that a policy of hostility toward dictators is unsuccessful. Usually it tends to strengthen the dictator and lead to retaliatory measures. To strengthen the democratic processes, the United States should rely—and does rely—on constant encouragement to dictators such as Franco to extend greater political liberty within their countries. Such methods pro-

During his time in Spain, Rubottom had numerous meetings with government officials, including General Francisco Franco. Above, Franco shakes hands with Rubottom. The tall man standing behind Franco in the photograph is American Ambassador John Davis Lodge.

duce results slowly, but they are the only methods that will ultimately succeed."

Charged with finding a way to reach accord with Spain, Dick oversaw, after much negotiation, the signing of the historic Pact of Madrid in 1953, an agreement that ended a long period of isolation for Spain. In *Spain and the United States Since World War II*, Dick writes:

> Given the polarization of opinion in the two countries with respect to each other, how did a policy of rapprochement materialize? The thawing of relations was a gradual process, an evolving series of initiatives. Each step was followed by a period of adjustment and consolidation. Increasingly, each nation needed the other.

Even so, there were plenty of roadblocks to the process. Along with U.S. allies in Europe, many Americans were angry about U.S. overtures to Spain.

However, Rubottom and Murphy note in their book that, by the war's end, it had become clear that Spain and the United States would each find mutual benefit in giving the other a fresh look. They note that in some ways the partnership between the two countries was unlikely. At that time, the U.S. was at the height of its power and prestige in the world, while Spain was suffering from ostracism by other countries. Up to that point, what Americans knew about Spain was unflattering—centering largely on the nation's civil war, which had lasted from 1936–1939. Too, Americans were aware of Spain's links to Axis powers during World War II.

Spanish citizens, for their part, viewed the United States as "an interloper in Latin America." In part, this was because Spaniards had hoped that Spain's *Hispanidad* Program would lead Latin America back to the fold of Spanish influence. Growing U.S. influence in Latin America threatened to thwart this goal.

Furthermore, in 1948, the United States government re-fused aid to Spain under the Marshall Plan, despite Spain's overwhelming need for such aid.

Rubottom notes that, "Despite all these barriers, the U.S. felt it was important to find some way to deal with Spain, because of the location of the Straits of Gibraltar, and also because of Spain's larger strategic location in the region. The United States had a direct security interest there. Through the Madrid Pact, we installed three airports for the U.S. Air Force and we also opened a naval base on the southernmost port, in Cadiz. We took plenty of criticism for these initiatives, but in the end we opened up trade and also protected our national security right there at the Mediterranean.

"As regards the American media, I sometimes felt as though journalists at home were always trying to pull the rug out from under us. We thought we were doing our job there, in accordance with the will of the executive and, if

During his time in Spain as a part of the USOM program, Dick and other officials watched as the first Santa Gertrudas cattle are unloaded at Barajas Airport in Madrid.

I'm any judge of opinion on the Hill, in accordance with the will of the Congress. Congress clearly supported our policy in Spain."

Even though newspapers in the U.S. weren't always supportive of diplomatic efforts in Spain and elsewhere, Rubottom continued to believe press freedom was essential. "To me, it's integral to the American way of life to have the *New York Times* tell us what it thinks about what we are doing. I suppose for every critical editorial that the *Times* may have run about our efforts in Spain or elsewhere, we'd have an editorial in the *New York Herald Tribune*, the *Washington Post*, the *Dallas News*, or some other paper that was applauding our efforts. We were very sensitive to what they had to say, both in the U.S. and abroad."

Rubottom believes that Spain allowed the U.S. strategic moves because they wanted the legitimacy of dealing with the United States. Secondly, the pact resulted in substantial U.S. monetary contributions to Spain's defense capabilities. And finally, Spain was on the U.S. side in the emerging Cold War. "Spain was strongly anti-Communist," Rubottom concludes.

On the personal front, Dick describes his years in Spain as a happy time. "Of all our posts, Spain was my favorite. First, of course, the job I was doing was important. In the end, I made our relations with Spain good. I was very close to the Ambassador at the time, whose name was James Plymouth Dunn. He was later replaced by John Davis Lodge."

Billy Ruth and the children also enjoyed living in Spain, Dick says. "Madrid was a wonderful place to live during those years. Our house there wasn't the best we ever lived in, but it was comfortable. It was very close to the big football stadium, and Madrid is crazy about football, or *futbol*, which we know in the U.S. as soccer. Whenever the Madrid team, known as Real Madrid, was playing, thousands of people would pour past our house to watch. Rick learned to play soccer when we lived there, and later, when he went to Phillips Exeter Academy, he played on his school team."

As they had in Bogotá, the children went to a British school, again with children from all around the world whose parents wanted them to take classes in English. As before, the children wore uniforms. Even today, Eleanor Rubottom Odden remains in contact with a Dutch and an American friend she made in Madrid at the British Institute.

Dick commented on the effectiveness of schools such as the British Institute in a speech given to the Strategic Intelligence School in Washington, D.C., on his return from Spain. "When we went to Spain in 1953," he said then, "the only English school that our children could attend was the one operated by the British Institute, which is a cultural arm of the British government. The school was similar to our Casa Americana schools. As many as 85% or 90% of the students were Spanish youngsters and there the British were able to bring the highest level of training and cultural opportunity to bear on growing Spanish children, who will probably be in important positions later in Spanish society."

As well as enjoying their school and the work Dick was doing, the family had a wonderful group of friends in Madrid—the Cromwells, the McClellands, the Bartons. All the fathers in these families were connected with the Embassy, and all the families had children. So the families would go on group picnics, or organize activities for the children—including a ballroom dance class for the older children.

When she was in seventh grade, Eleanor transferred to the American Dependents School, which was operated by the U.S. military.

The family attended services at the Anglican Church in Madrid every Sunday. Dick and Billy Ruth organized the Sunday School program there, and procured the study materials for it. In addition, Billy Ruth organized Bluebirds and Cub Scout groups for Eleanor and Rick, as well as play groups for toddler John. Thus, despite the fact that the family was living in a society under an absolute ruler, life was rich and full.

Dick remembers Franco as a "stern, hard dictator. But I don't think there was a lot of brutality shown to people who opposed him." Even so, when asked during those years whether he spoke Spanish, Dick always replied, *"Yo puedo defenderme,"* which means, "I can defend myself."

When the family lived in Silver Spring, Maryland, they had a close group of neighborhood friends. This photo is inscribed "Just so you will never forget February 13, 1953. Jane and Meff."

At the end of his tenure in Spain, Dick reflected on the period of his life in a speech titled "The Development of United States Foreign Policy." He gave this speech only four months after leaving Spain, and in it he provided a studied response to diplomatic efforts during the previous four years.

"I think the United States policy in Spain over the last few years is a classic example of the pressures that are brought to bear on the United States," he said, "and [these pressures] result ultimately in the formulation of a policy, then in the change in that policy, and then in the redirection again of a policy. Now, I'm not going back through the centuries to tell you about the role that Spain has played in the western hemisphere. You know it was important. But, of course, we had the war with Spain at the end of the last century which effectively meant the end of Spain as an empire and as a great nation. Spain has never been the same since and never will be the same, and yet the fact that we are able to do today what we are doing in Spain is a remarkable commentary on the flexibility of the usually described inflexible, stolid, patient, all-suffering Spaniard, because I think there would have to be some popular support for our presence in Spain even with the Franco government, in order for it to be maintained and to advance the way our presence is being advanced by the construction of [military] bases there, and so forth."

Rubottom holds, however, that from the Spanish-American War onward there has always been a dictatorship in Spain. He points to the monarchy and then to the "tight little group" that tried to run the Spanish Republic in the 1930s.

"In 1936," he went on in the speech, "when Franco decided to revolt and brought most of the army with him, [the result was] probably one of the bloodiest civil wars that's ever been fought anywhere (except the one in the United

States), lasting from 1936 to 1939. You had approximately 1/21 or 1/22 of the whole Spanish Republic wiped out and more than a million lives lost, and the scars of that war are still being felt, believe you me.

"In 1939, just on the outbreak of the war in Europe—what became World War II—Franco was finally successful, and he merged with the government. His government is still in power. It is supported primarily by the military, the Church, by the *Falange* [the name assigned to several Spanish political movements in the 1930s, especially the original fascist movement], by the economic and financial oligarchy, which is very, very important. There are other influences of one kind or another, but I would say these are the principal pillars of the Franco Government . . . As you know, Herbert Matthews of the *New York Times* has written a series of articles just this week . . . [because] Spain is a subject that has [evoked] violent opinion throughout the United States during this modern period, much of it strongly against Spain. I don't think I can recall ever having been influenced by propaganda, as an adult, to the extent that I was during the time of the fighting of the Spanish Civil War from 1936 to 1939. *Time* magazine, *Harper's*, all of the newspapers, practically anything that you read, was slanted just about 100% in support of the Republican forces and against Franco. So the stage was set here for the complete revulsion to Franco when he took over, and that revulsion did take place. Franco's role in World War II didn't help. As you know, he was neutral and he made some statements which, quoted by themselves, certainly are enough to damn anybody who fought against the Germans, the Italians and the Japanese. But nevertheless, he remained neutral. There was active cooperation going on with the United States that some of you know about. During nearly all of that time Franco kept the Germans out, and I suppose Hitler has never had a rage such as that he had on the October day in 1940 when he met Franco at Hendaye, in the railroad station there, and got turned down in his effort to cross the Spanish peninsula on his way to Africa. I think there is not sufficient recognition of the Spanish role as a neutral in World War II.

"We came out of World War II and, of course, in 1945-46 we had a completely different situation insofar as our relations with the Soviet Union were concerned. The United Nations was established and had its first meeting and one of its first items of business was to pass the resolution that, in effect, severed diplomatic relations between virtually all the important countries and Spain. That lasted for four years. The Spanish bitterly resented it at the time. It came after they had knocked themselves out in their own civil war, and then had been denied access to the world markets during World War II. They might have had a chance to recuperate, but they were diplomatically embargoed. They are still not members of the World Bank or the IMF (International Monetary Fund) and that was the situation that we were up against in 1950.

"Finally, public opinion began to swing around. There were subtle influences at work, certainly the Catholic Church here at home. The great figures in public life in the Catholic Church have, I think, always been more tolerant of Franco and I think their influence was beginning to be felt. There has always been strong opposition to Spain on the part of labor. Laborers have been actively and publicly against Spain, but some of their opposition apparently began to dissipate. Then there was debate over on the Hill and there has been remarkable unanimity of opinion in the Congress, that as the issues became more clearly drawn—and this problem more than anything else had to do with the change between ourselves and the Communist world—that we couldn't do without Spain.

"So in 1950 we restored full diplomatic relations with Spain, as did most of the other governments of the western free world that had engaged in this so-called embargo, and from there one thing led to another. Admiral Sherman [Admiral Forrest P. Sherman, Chief of U.S. Naval Operations] went to Spain, I believe, at the end of 1950. As far as I know, his mission at the time was secret, but he engaged in discussions with Franco, and for all practical purposes got a commitment which led to the negotiating teams going over in February of 1952, when we started the long drawn-out negotiations with Spain that were finally culminated in 1953, September 26, with the signing of a military defense agreement which led to the base program—a military assistance program providing Franco with equipment on a grant basis and the economic aid program that has provided them with considerable economic aid. I was in charge of the Economic Aid Program during the last year and a half I was there, so I will mention one additional point, further to point out the degree to which we are getting cooperation from Spain. They, perhaps through ignorance, through desire to be brought back into the respectable arena, if you please, maybe agreed to things that were counter-productive to them. They might have gotten a better agreement if they had held out longer, I don't know. But on the economic side, all the Marshall Plan countries put up a dollar's worth of their own currency for every dollar of economic aid they got—lira, francs, whatever it might be. In turn, we kept 10% of the currency for our own expenses and then plowed 90% of the local currency back into the economic development or the reconstruction of the war-torn countries with that money so that, in effect, we were getting almost two dollars worth of value out of each dollar of the aid program—a dollar's worth of foreign exchange to buy the stuff that was shipped over in the form of railroad equipment, electric power plants, etc., and then a dollar's worth of local currency to construct and to build and to modernize, etc.

"In the case of Spain, the agreement is on a much different basis. We keep the usual 10% for government expenditures and then we apply 60% of the balance to the cost of the base construction program, so that Spain is directly participating in the cost, or contributing to the cost, of the bases in Spain by putting up 60% of the pesetas that they pay in for each dollar of economic aid. That leaves 30% (10%, 60%, 30%). What happens to the remaining 30%? The 30% is used to improve the transportation system linking the bases, the highways and the railroads, and we tell them, in effect, where that money is spent.

"So we have gotten a remarkably good deal out of the Spaniards. The cooperation on the whole has been good. You can see that I feel strongly that it's a good program, and I think that in this moment of crisis we are putting Spain to the test. So far, she has held out pretty well. Spain would like very much to be a bridge between the Western world and the Arab nations and she is really up against it now where the test is being applied because of the Suez Canal crisis and her desire, I am sure, to stay on more or less speaking terms, at least, with Nasser [Gamal Abdel Nasser, president of Egypt]. But so far I think Spain has played a constructive role. She was admitted to the United Nations this last year, and all in all I feel we have accomplished a tremendous comeback . . .

"The first of the bases—the one near Madrid called Torrejon—will probably be operable, too, within the next few months. It's a tremendous base. And then there is a big naval installation called Rota that will take ships of all kinds. When it's finished, it will be able to handle aircraft and carriers, etc. [Naval Station Rota, Spain is strategically located near the Straits of Gibraltar and at the halfway point between the United States and Southwest Asia.]

There may be other bases in the future, although the Spaniards are beginning to get educated and they are exacting a tougher price in the negotiations as we move along, but that is to be expected. I think the results in the future of the degree of cooperation as the chips are down, as in this particular power play that's on right now with Nasser, will depend in large measure on whether we are willing to pay that price."

Whenever possible—whether home on leave, or living in Washington on assignment—Dick and Billy Ruth drove with the children to Texas so Eleanor Ann, Ricky and John could visit their aunts, uncles and cousins. They would see Billy Ruth's family in Corsicana: her parents, Anna and Frank Young; her sister, Mary Jo David and her husband Lewis and their boys, John and Dick David; her brother Maurice and his wife, Eleanor, and their son, Bill. Billy's sister, Anna Mae, and her husband George and their children, George, Ann, and James, would come from Midland while the Rubottoms were in Texas, and her eldest sister, Tillie Frances, and her husband, Frank Nagle, along with their boys, Fred and Frank, would come from Austin.

The Rubottoms also took every opportunity to visit Dick's family. Nancy Merle Lea and her husband, Willis, lived in Dallas with their three children, Nancy, Richard and Robert. Martha Frances and her husband, Ernest Johnson, lived in Dublin, Texas, with children Beth, Ernest, Jr., Dick, Joy, Jack and Tim. Family gatherings were large and spirited, and all the Rubottoms looked forward to reunions with loved ones.

On one visit to Dallas, while the family was living in Spain, the following article appeared in the *Dallas Morning News*:

The Rubottoms visited family in Texas before leaving for Spain. 1953.

Bull Fights First
Spanish Soccer Gains Followers

by Helen Bullock

Bullfighting still has a tremendous hold on the people of Spain, but the game of soccer, or *"futbol,"* is running it a close second, an American diplomat, Roy Richard Rubottom, reported here Thursday.

In Madrid, which has been home to Rubottom and his family for two years, soccer games each weekend fill a stadium that holds 125,000 persons, he said.

Rubottom conceded he personally likes to watch bullfights, but said he has not become an aficionado—the Spaniard's word for a fellow who takes his bullfighting or football very seriously.

A native Texan, Rubottom has been in the foreign service of the United States Department of State for seven years.

On vacation, he is visiting in the home of his sister, Mrs. Willis Lea Jr., 3534 Colgate.

Rubottom has two titles: Director of United States Operations Missions to Spain, and Counselor of the Embassy for Economic Affairs.

Of Spain's economy—devastated by a long civil war and then paralyzed tradewise by World War II, though Spain remained neutral in that big conflict—Rubottom said:

"She (Spain) is on the way up. She hasn't any other way to go."

The booming tourist trade has helped Spain financially and accounts for 20 percent of all the country's dollar trade, he said. And Dallas supplies its share of the turistas.

"You'd be surprised how many Dallas people visit in Spain.

A bunch of Dallas oilmen are even exploring Spain for oil," he said.

Also helping Spain to get back on her feet, of course, is this country's program of economic aid which began in 1953.

Like Texas, though, Spain has its drought troubles. And 60 percent of the Spanish people work in agriculture.

So serious was the drought in 1953 that it took all of the American aid dollars, about 85 million of them, to import enough wheat to feed the Spanish people. Normally Spain produces enough wheat to supply its own needs.

The water shortage hurts Spain electrically, too, since most of its power is hydroelectric.

As for living in Spain, it is especially interesting to a family which has spent years in other Spanish-speaking countries, said Rubottom.

His assignments have taken him and his family to Colombia, Paraguay, Mexico, and Venezuela. [Editor's note: The family never lived in Venezuela.]

It was easy, said Rubottom, to adjust to Spain's three-hour "lunch hours" and to eating dinner at 10:30 p.m.

It is the custom in Madrid, he said, for stores and offices to open about 10 a.m. and close from 1:30 to 4:30 p.m. They reopen at 4:30 and stay open until 8:30 p.m.

Not everyone gets to take a siesta, though. Most everybody goes home for lunch, and for many workers the long ride by bus or subway does not leave time for a nap, even with a 3-hour lunch period.

About 1,600,000 persons live in Madrid, in an area about the size of Dallas, said Rubottom.

It is a city of apartment dwellers. Most of the apartment buildings are six to eight stories high, of pink brick trimmed in white limestone.

Rubottom described Spain as "a real bastion against Communism."

Contracts are now being let, he reported, for America's four air bases and Navy base to be built in Spain.

Rubottom will return to Madrid next month with his wife and their three children, Eleanor Ann, 11; Frank Richard, 9; and John William, 2.

CHAPTER 8

1956–1961

Things had gone well for the Rubottoms in Spain. In fact, Dick's negotiations there were so successful that his name was suggested for a position as Director of Economic Mission in Korea. This was right after the Korean War, a highly uncertain period in U.S.–Korean relations, and thus the job was another very important one. Dick was considering the position even though it wasn't in Latin America.

As he was pondering his options, however, he received a call from an old friend and colleague, the prominent Texas attorney Henry F. Holland. Holland, who was from San Antonio, was serving at that time as Assistant Secretary of State for Inter-American Affairs in Washington, having replaced John Moors Cabot in March 1954. Holland had written to invite Dick to come and work with him as his Deputy.

After giving it considerable thought, and conferring with Billy Ruth, Dick concluded that he would be most effective if he stayed within his purview, which of course was Latin America. He decided to accept Holland's offer.

So once again the family pulled up stakes and moved to Washington, this time into the Wesley Heights neighborhood of Northwest Washington. Although the neighborhood schools were good—especially on the elementary level—

Top, left:
Correspondence with officials, family, and friends required significant time.

Below, left: When they lived in Washington, D.C., the Rubottoms were featured in a newspaper profile. Here they're pictured tending the family garden.

Below, right: For the same article, the photographer caught the family playing a game of Scrabble in the den of their home.

Dick and Billy Ruth decided that their two older children would attend private school. Eleanor, by then an eighth grader, enrolled in The Potomac School, where she completed eighth and ninth grades. Then she went to The Madeira School, a private girls' school in McLean, Virginia, for grades ten through twelve. Madeira is located only twelve miles from Washington, so Eleanor commuted as a day student for as long as the family remained in Washington. When she was a senior, her father was named Ambassador to Argentina, and Dick and Billy Ruth, along with John, moved to Buenos Aires. At that point, Eleanor became a boarder at Madeira.

During those same years, Rick Rubottom was enrolled at Landon School, an independent, non-sectarian school for boys. Landon was founded in 1929 in a converted mansion in the heart of Washington's embassy row. When the Rubottoms moved to Argentina, Rick went to Phillips Exeter in Exeter, New Hampshire, where he boarded.

John, meanwhile, as the youngest child in the family, attended the neighborhood elementary school in Washington until he moved with his parents to South America.

While it's undeniable that many U.S. diplomats have family connections or wealth, this was never true of the Rubottoms. Whatever success Dick enjoyed was the result of his determination, hard work, and fundamental integrity. Also, of course, he was highly intelligent and had the patience and listening ear necessary for effective negotiation. He was gifted, in other words, but far from wealthy. It can't have been easy, therefore, for him and Billy Ruth to send two children to expensive private schools.

According to Eleanor, "Sending Rick and me to private schools was a huge commitment for my parents. I think they felt they were giving us the opportunity to have the best education possible. Education was a huge value for them, and one that they were willing to sacrifice for."

An irony of Dick's decision to move back to Washington at Henry Holland's behest was that, very soon after they arrived, on September 13, 1956, Holland himself resigned his position as Assistant Secretary of State for Inter-American Affairs. With that, Dick was catapulted into position as Acting Assistant Secretary of State for Inter-American Affairs, a position he held for nine months before himself being confirmed Assistant Secretary of State for Inter-American Affairs on June 18, 1957, where he remained until August 27, 1960.

Rubottom recalls how his designation to the permanent position came about. "I had been Acting Assistant Secretary for half a year. One afternoon I was riding in the back seat of a car with John Foster Dulles, who of course was Secretary of State during the Eisenhower administration.

"Secretary Dulles turned to me and said, 'By the way, Dick, I'm recommending to the President today that you be named Assistant Secretary of State for Inter-American Affairs.'

"He caught me off-guard. I said, 'Well, Mr. Dulles, I'm honored. But I'm sure a lot of people want that position.'

"He barked, 'Rubottom, do you want the job or not?'

"'Yes, sir,' I answered. This was in April, and the following June I was confirmed."

Asked what held up his confirmation, Rubottom replies,

"There were other people angling for the job, and I think frankly Mr. Dulles didn't want any of them in place, so he just waited them out."

In his book titled *The Wine Is Bitter*, Milton Eisenhower, Dwight Eisenhower's brother, writes of the period in September 1956 when the first meeting of the twenty-one presidential representatives of the American republics was scheduled to be held in Washington D.C.

"As the representative of the President of the host country," Eisenhower writes, "I would be chairman of the group." Then he writes:

Dick succeeded his old friend Henry Holland as Assistant Secretary of State for Inter-American Affairs in 1957. Here they are discussing the transition of power.

Secretary of State John Foster Dulles congratulates Rubottom on becoming Assistant Secretary of State for Inter-American Affairs. June 19, 1957.

The family congratulates Dick on his new position as Assistant Secretary of State for Inter-American Affairs. (left à right) Eleanor Ann, Billy Ruth, Dick holding John, Secretary Dulles, Dick's mother, Eleanor.

Henry Holland, who with President Eisenhower and me had conceived the whole idea of this new effort to strengthen the Organization of American States and have it work for individual betterment, suddenly announced that he would resign as Assistant Secretary of State for Inter-American Affairs to enter private business in New York. He simply could not afford financially to remain in government.

I was frustrated. Holland had carefully thought through the types of problems we should bring up and that the other representatives were likely to raise. He had been in communication with our ambassadors in all of the countries and was better prepared to counsel than anyone else. At my urging, he promised to come to Washington often during the months in which the presidential representatives would be working, but he would no longer have an influential voice in Latin-American affairs.

His Deputy Assistant Secretary of State was Roy R. Rubottom, Jr., one of the ablest and most forthright men I have ever known. Rubottom was bilingual and knew Latin America thoroughly. He had served in several of the republics and had also been head of our economic mission in Spain before coming to Washington as Holland's deputy. He was rather young, governmentally speaking (forty-four at the time); I suppose this is why he was named Acting Assistant Secretary, for he surely had all the talents and leadership qualities the post demanded. This was a most unfortunate arrangement at the very time that a crucial international conference, which presumably was to blaze new trails, was about to get underway. Henry Holland could do no more than give me personal help. Rubottom, only Acting, could not launch out into new areas and policies—an "acting," as Washington knows, never can. So from the moment the conference opened, it was almost a foregone conclusion that we would have to develop ideas and programs within current policy. Had things worked out differently, it is conceivable that this meeting would have spelled out the great revision of United States policy which was so desperately needed and which was soon to come.

Dick was intrigued by John Foster Dulles and his brother, Allen W. Dulles, who was head of the CIA at that time. "The brothers had enormous influence in Washington in the late 1950s," he says. "I wasn't close to John Foster Dulles, but I knew him well. I thought he was a very effective administrator. I remember Dulles as a bright and able, but somewhat stern, man. He was not an affable personality. He had been a prominent Wall Street lawyer before he became Secretary of State. He hadn't had previous State Department experience when he and Allen came into government, but the brothers were both plenty successful, and they had money to keep their families going. As with most appointments of that type, they simply had a desire to serve. They were strong personalities, and they were always controversial in the public eye.

"John Foster Dulles died of cancer while I was still Assistant Secretary of Inter-American Affairs, and his obituary tells the story of his service to the nation. The Dulles brothers' service ended after the Eisenhower administration."

"After Dulles' death, I served under Christian A. Herter," Rubottom recalls. "Herter was a non-career appointee from Massachusetts, who served from April of 1959, when Dulles resigned because of illness, until January 20, 1961."

As history unfolded, the months Dick Rubottom served as Acting Assistant Secretary were critical ones in U.S.-Latin American affairs. He says, "If I had it to do over again, one of the things that I would do is that I would never willingly go along with being Acting Assistant Secretary for nine months, as I was. This greatly diminished the authority of my office and deprived me of some of the influence that I should have had, even after I was finally confirmed as Assistant Secretary. I consider this a very, very serious blunder, because more than anything else it tended to downgrade the importance of Latin-American affairs. I was Acting Assistant Secretary from mid-September of 1956 until April 1957, and I wasn't confirmed until the following June. Altogether that's a period of about nine months during which the United States didn't have a fully authorized Assistant Secretary. I should have gotten out of that spot much sooner."

Asked what he views as his most significant contributions during that period, Rubottom says, "Well, to begin with, the

(left to right) Secretary Herter, Assistant Secretary Rubottom, Horacio Lafer, Brazilian Ambassador Walt Salles.

role that I played in the formulation of the Inter-American Bank, in the negotiation and chartering of the institution, was key. I was witness to and participant in all of that."

The Inter-American Development Bank, or IDB, was formally created in 1959, when the Special Advisory Commission of the Inter-American Economic and Social Council of the OAS met in order to draft the Articles of Agreement establishing the bank.

In the months leading up to that, Rubottom made a number of speeches in support of the IDB. In one, he wrote, "The bank's exclusive attention to Latin America will assure the most sympathetic possible consideration of the needs of those countries for additional public capital. More emphasis will be placed on wider investment of private capital in Latin America, which in turn will promote economic progress in Latin America. With the strains upon the budget of the United States for its many commitments throughout the world, and with severe needs in many Latin-American countries, the investment of capital needed for economic growth there must depend in large measure upon the great resources of private enterprise."

On December 30, 1959, the agreement to form the bank was ratified by eighteen countries, including Argentina, Bolivia, Brazil, Chile, Colombia, Costa Rica, Dominican Republic, Ecuador, El Salvador, Guatemala, Haití, Honduras, Mexico, Nicaragua, Panama, Paraguay, Peru and the United States.

The bank's initial resources of $1 billion meant that Latin American nations would have a potential new source of financing for worthy projects. In 1961, Rubottom wrote, "After only two years in business, [the IDB] has loaned more than $650 million. It has just voted an increase in capital to $2 billion at its annual meeting in Caracas. The Bank has also successfully offered its bonds for public subscription in Europe and the United States."

Rubottom continues, "There were so many problematic matters in Latin America while I was in that office. The United States had increasingly difficult attitudes to address as we steered through these events."

Among the diplomatic landmines he helped negotiate were those involving:

- Marcos Evangelista Pérez Jiménez, a soldier who was President of Venezuela from 1952 to 1958, and who was ousted in a bloodless coup in 1958.
- The people of the Dominican Republic, who were suffering under the brutal dictatorship of Rafael Trujillo, as they had since 1930, while their leader amassed a great fortune. However, Trujillo welcomed U.S. businesses and maintained a pro-U.S. foreign policy. The

Today, the IDB continues to help Latin-American countries grow and thrive. According to the bank's Web site, its influence is ever expanding. In fact:

- The Bank provides more financing to Latin America and the Caribbean than any other government-owned regional financial institution.
- It underwent a major overhaul in recent years, connecting with new clients and putting more personnel in country offices.
- A big debt-cancellation program for its five poorest members (Bolivia, Guyana, Haiti, Honduras and Nicaragua) is financed entirely by the Bank itself.
- The IDB turns 50 in 2009.
- Countries that receive IDB financing also hold a majority of its shares.
- The portfolio of projects under consideration numbers more than 600.*

*http://www.iadb.org/aboutus/Fivethings.cfm?language=English

United States supported his anti-Communist stance in Latin America.

- Anastasio Somoza Garcia, the Nicaraguan dictator, was supported by the United States because he, too, was staunchly anti-Communist. But Somoza was assassinated in 1956, which led to instability in the region.
- Juan Perón of Argentina, who had come into power through a coup in 1943, was kicked out of office just before Dick came back to Washington, so that Dick and other U.S. diplomats had to work with the transition government.

"The list of challenges was long," Dick recalls, "and all were complicated and difficult. Even so, I think we managed them reasonably well. It's important to remember that the main issue for the United States in the world at that time was to counter Communist ideology, which sometimes meant that we formed alliances with leaders whose tactics we couldn't support. It was a fine line to walk.

"But surely the most pressing challenge of all in those years involved the changes of leadership and government in Cuba. Fulgencio Batista, who was the military leader of Cuba in the early 1940s, had staged a successful military coup in 1952, and most Cubans were ashamed of that event. Cuba was undergoing great change, and in response the Batista government became more and more repressive as the decade passed.

"By 1957, dictators had been mowed down in Latin America—Rojas Pinilla was forced out in Colombia; Magloire fell in Haiti; Lozano tumbled in Honduras. Somoza was assassinated in Nicaragua. Then came the ouster of Pérez Jiménez over the New Year 1958 in Venezuela."

Rubottom says that by the late 1950s, Batista's leadership was challenged by a young revolutionary named Fidel

Castro. "Fidel Castro was highly charismatic, and he was respected in some quarters because he was an outspoken critic of Batista, whose leadership of Cuba had become increasingly despotic," Rubottom recalls.

"When Fidel Castro landed on the shores of Eastern Cuba on November 30, 1956, the winds of change were already blowing strongly throughout Latin America. Perón had fallen in Argentina. Odría, seeing the handwriting on the wall, had turned over the reins of government to a democratically elected successor in Peru.

"Castro built a large following in Cuba," Rubottom says of that time, "and he began efforts to seize control of the government. We supported Batista in that conflict, but I have always maintained that Castro could not have been described as a Communist at that point in his political career. Not really."

Rubottom notes that, with the developing revolution in Cuba, the United States was impaled on the horns of a dilemma. It was pressured by both sides to intervene in revolt-torn Cuba. "Our government certainly did not condone the repressive tactics of the Batista government," he recalls, "and the U.S. deplored the increasing signs that Batista would not permit free elections to be held in mid-1958 to choose his successor. On the other hand, the U.S. could not condone the violent, utterly destructive revolution being led by Castro, especially in view of the doubts regarding his political leanings, and the known Communist ties of several of his closest collaborators, including his brother, Raul Castro, and Che Guevara."

Rubottom says the United States took its stand on the principle of dignity and freedom for the individual, and government by the consent of the governed. He goes on, "This, of course, was not a popular position with either side in Cuba. The Cubans seemed to forget that they had been among the most outspoken in demanding that the United

States give up its policy of intervening in Latin-American affairs three decades before. The U.S. was committed to this policy and was destined to go through a very trying experience for the next six years as the Castro government, once it came into power, continually charged its larger neighbor with intervention while blatantly intervening in the affairs of four or five of its immediate neighbors through attempted invasions, and all of its neighbors through propaganda and outright subversion.

"My own doubts regarding Castro were many, but principally I distrusted his revolution, in spite of its stated aims, because of his wholly destructive approach to change. From his statements it was becoming increasingly clear that he felt that everything in Cuba, even some of the good things, would have to be destroyed in order to build his 'new Cuba.' I did not hesitate to express my doubts to those who were in any position to influence public opinion, as was reported in the *Washington Daily News* on February 3, 1961. A story written by the editor of that paper, John O'Rourke, said, 'Mr. Rubottom warned newsmen about Castro at the time . . . Mr. Rubottom knew the score on Castro, and gave many newspapers Castro's background.'"

In September 1960, Rubottom and his family left Washington for Argentina, where Dick Rubottom was to serve as U.S. Ambassador. Events in Cuba, however, continued to dog him.

"The tragedy, I think, came with the way that the United States ultimately bungled through the Cuban operation of 1961," Rubottom says. "I'm not attempting to assess blame, but this situation was a tragedy, and our relations with Cuba suffered from it. It's quite significant that the whole O.A.S. eventually took sanctions against Cuba, and these remained in effect for many years. I believe everybody except Mexico withdrew relations or severed relations with Cuba."

What Rubottom is referring to here, of course, is the infamous Bay of Pigs Invasion. This operation was an unsuccessful attempt, by a force of Cuban exiles who had been trained by the U.S. military, to invade southern Cuba and force the overthrow of Fidel Castro. The invasion was planned and funded by the U.S. in 1960, and it was launched in April 1961, only three months after John F. Kennedy assumed the U.S. presidency. The Cuban armed forces, in turn, had been trained by Eastern Bloc nations, and those forces defeated the invasion troops within three days.

Although Rubottom was in Argentina during these events, he continued to closely observe matters in Cuba. He says, "As you know, this effort aborted for quite a number of reasons. I've always felt that one of the reasons was the undue publicity that it was given in advance, so that everything that was being done was being published in the newspapers in Miami and New York, almost in real time.

Rubottom asks, "What were the options that the United States had in the spring of 1961? It could have called off the invasion attempt, insofar as its support was concerned. It could have postponed the attempt. It could have committed enough support to the attempt to guarantee that it would be successful, and this was the basis on which the plan was originally drawn up—*the only basis*. Or it could go ahead and provide half-hearted support to the 1,200 Cubans who had been trained at great expense and at great risk. The last option was the worst option, and this was the one that the United States chose to follow. The President's decision *not* to support the Bay of Pigs invasion with whatever necessary to assure its success and thus bring the downfall of Castro communism in Cuba did more than simply endanger the lives of 1,200 anti-Communists and eighteen months' planning. It also foreclosed virtually all other options except for 'living with' a communist-dominated

Cuba which, no matter how much harassed by U.S. economic sanctions, could exist with the U.S.S.R. aid program.

"I think we should have thrown all the guns we had into trying to get Batista to move sooner than he did, instead of relying on those rather inadequate and ill-prepared men who were there."

With the failure of the Bay of Pigs, U.S.–Cuba relations deteriorated precipitously, which chain of events led, the following year, to the Cuban Missile Crisis.

CHAPTER 9

In His Own Words: Reflections on Cuba

Some years after the events described above—notably those involving Cuba, the Dominican Republic, and other pivotal Latin-American countries—Dick Rubottom was visited by a scholar named John Luter, who interviewed him about his years in the State Department. That interview is now in the collection of President Dwight David Eisenhower's papers at Columbia University in New York. The interview has only been lightly edited, because it was the hope of scholars at Columbia that the tone would be conversational, forthright, and honest. Notes about the main players appear in brackets, in context, throughout the section. The interview was conducted in 1970, and this chapter should be read with that time frame in mind.

Q: Now, throughout that time trouble was developing in Cuba, and throughout 1958, we pretty much followed a policy of non-intervention, or tried to. I believe in March 1958 we suspended delivery of arms to Batista. How good was our intelligence during that period, on the nature of the Castro movement? Any thoughts on that?

RUBOTTOM: Yes, the Castro movement was developing all during that time. The landing was on November 30, 1956. The fighting was sort of quiescent in '57, and of course it began to pick up in '58, and as you say, in March we put the ban on the shipment of arms [to Batista]. I think it had to do with 2,000 rifles. Incidentally, one of these days perhaps I will put down in my book, if I ever write it: that decision [to ban the arms shipment] was made when I was away from Washington. I was away on leave and I heard it on the radio. I stopped my car and called back to my deputy to ask him if this were so, and he said yes. Of course, a decision that important had to be approved by much higher authority than the Acting Assistant Secretary, but because I was away, he was acting . . . This was a rather key decision, and I can understand that its denial, even though the amount was small, represented a political psychological setback to Batista.

Now, you asked about our intelligence. I would say that our intelligence was fair. I met once a week with my opposite number in the CIA who was in charge of all their Latin-American section, and [we were always] trying to identify Castro [ideologically] and put a label on him. We really tried very hard, but it was not possible to label him as a Communist then. And the only 20-20 hindsight types who have called him a well-known Communist then were some of the rather reactionary people, [as] I choose to call them, in this country, who took as gospel whatever Trujillo or Batista had in their files.

But [whether Castro started out as a Communist] is a tough question, and [along with] whatever we got from the CIA, the embassy and others, we had to contend with what was published in the *New York Times*. As you know, that newspaper is considered something of a voice for the United States. Herbert Matthews [*New York Times* reporter who revealed that Fidel Castro was still alive and hiding in the Sierra Maestra Mountains of Cuba after Batista had publicly declared that Castro had been killed], after he went to the hills and talked with Castro sometime in 1957 and wrote his series, had built Castro into sort of Robin Hood type, to the point where [Castro] had heroic proportion in the minds of many people, including [some] people in the United States who . . . in those days looked upon him as the darling of the anti-dictators, the anti-Batista.

Q: What effect on the State Department thinking did the Matthews articles have?

RUBOTTOM: Well, they never did have very much effect

With President Eisenhower. 1959.

on my thinking. I knew Herbert Matthews. I used to talk to
him on the phone occasionally. It was very important that
I talk to him . . . Let me tell you why it was important.
Herbert Matthews was on the editorial board of the *New
York Times*, and I can remember when I first became
Assistant Secretary, he had the chief of the editorial board
invite me up to lunch, and I went into the sanctum-
sanctorum of the *Times* and had lunch with these five or six
people who write the editorials for the *Times* . . . Then,
later on, Matthews used to call me every time he got ready
to write an editorial—he'd call me about what was happening in Bolivia or Haiti.

So I was amazed, frankly, at the extent to which a lot of
the *New York Times* editorials reflected my own views, after
I would talk to Matthews. He listened on many things. But
as far as Cuba was concerned, he wasn't the listener, he was
the talker. And I'll have to admit that I had a pretty heavy
bias in my mind against Castro all the time, because his
whole approach to development and his approach to change
in a country was and is destructive. It's the revolutionary
approach in the real sense of the term, in contrast to the
evolutionary approach; instead of the constructive approach, and difficult though it might have been to evolve
things through the evolutionary method in Cuba, I still
think that is the way things should have been done, because
Cuba was not all bad. The whole country did not have to
be leveled in order to turn it around. It had one of the highest economic standards, in spite of under-employment
and all of the other problems that we know, and if suasion
had been brought to bear, perhaps things wouldn't have become so polarized, [with the two sides being] between
Batista, through a rational approach to have elections in
1958, and [Batista stepping] aside. Things might have been
different.

Q: Were efforts made by the State Department or others?

RUBOTTOM: Yes, that was our constant effort, and I say that we did not have effective ambassadors there at the time. One of them, Arthur Gardner, was there probably until . . . it must have been the spring or summer of 1957, and I might say here, in passing, that Earl E. T. Smith, who took his place, was the only ambassador who was appointed to a country in Latin America about whom I was not consulted in advance. I will never forget going up to Secretary Dulles's office one day and being told that Gardner was out and that Earl E. T. Smith was going to take his place. I was dumbfounded because, of course, that country was extremely important. Castro was already fighting in the hills, and to have made this kind of appointment without any consultation with those of us who were professionally involved, at my level, let alone below me—I thought it was rather unusual, to put it mildly.

Now, I want to go back and pick up the point about Ambassador Smith and the *New York Times*. One of the points that Smith makes in his book, *The Fourth Floor*, which is very critical of me personally and others, has to do with our suggestion that he go to New York to talk to Herbert Matthews. Well, the truth of the matter is that someone else suggested this to Smith before he was appointed, and he asked us if we thought this was a good idea and we said we thought it was. And I still think that for a man who was going to be Ambassador to Cuba to know the person who was writing about Cuba more than any other single writer in the United States, whether or not he agreed with him, was extremely important. Instead, well, Smith tried to turn this around and show it as a contrary, or adverse, picture of the kind of people we were in the State Department. I don't follow that line of reasoning at all.

Q: How did Smith happen to be appointed?

RUBOTTOM: I just don't know. He was wealthy man. He was a graduate of Yale. I think he had been an NCAA champion boxer. He'd made a fortune, I think as a stockbroker. He had been married two or three times, and I think took a very lovely lady with him as either his third or his fourth wife to Cuba. She has since died. Incidentally, she was a very bright woman. We all respected her very much, from what we could see of her meeting her socially before they went down there, and she played a very prominent part in the direction and even the political orientation of that embassy, and I think there were quite a few people near the ambassador who felt that she drafted many of the telegrams and so on that came back from there while he was there.

I can only say that as a good hard-boiled conservative, if not a reactionary out of the financial community, and one who had contributed to the party, there must have been someone who thought that this was the kind of man we needed there. He was certainly no namby-pamby, as Arthur Gardner had been, who had really almost made a fool of himself in the way he had scratched Batista's back, you know, and tried to curry favor with him.

Smith turned out to be a problem, too, but a problem of a different kind, and this, in a way, is tragic to think about. During those critical years, having two ill-prepared people there, no matter how honorable their intentions or how fine their loyalty to their country undoubtedly was. They were simply not the skilled type of diplomat that we needed in a situation of that kind.

Q: You say that Smith turned out to be a problem of a different kind. In what sense?

RUBOTTOM: Well, when Smith went down there, he was very conscious, after his briefing sessions, of the problems that Gardner had faced. He knew, of course, that Batista was going into a very critical time, if not into decline. That was mid-1957. He [Smith] was determined not to make the mistake that Gardner had, so he bent over backwards to avoid treating Batista the same effusive way that his predecessor had. He made a trip, Smith did, around Cuba within the first thirty or sixty days after he arrived, and when he got to Santiago, on the eastern end of the island, an incident occurred which I think greatly influenced his whole term as ambassador there.

A group of women was parading down the main street of the town dressed in black. I believe the firemen and the policemen used a water hose on these women to try to get them off the street. This made a very strong impression on Smith, and he had a normal and very human reaction, by which he deplored that this action had been taken against these women. He used the word "deplore." . . . This was the strongest word in his statement. This was considered by Batista and his lieutenants to be hypercritical commentary, and the editor of one of the leading newspapers . . . suggested that the Cuban government ought to ask for Smith's withdrawal and declare him *persona non grata*.

Naturally Smith was shocked by this reaction on the part of the Cubans. Nothing came of the suggestion that he be declared *persona non grata* . . . but anyway it succeeded in pulling Smith back. He was determined that he was not going to fall into a laudatory role toward Batista. Well, he got his fingers burned on this incident. He pulled back from any exposure at all, as a sort of neutral person, and eventually he pretty well closed himself off from the people in the Embassy who were trying to tell him what was happening in the country. I think later, in his book, he described many of them [the Embassy people] as pro-Castro. I suppose when a country's going through a revolution of that kind, it's hard to avoid taking sides. It's very hard to be objective in your estimate of the political situation.

But by the time Castro took office, in early 1959, Smith had gotten himself back into a position as pro-Batista and intensely anti-Castro, and had cut himself off from Embassy advice, as I say. Now in retrospect you might say, 'Well, doesn't that make him dead right, if he was anti-Castro?' I think it depends on what your public position is at a time like that. You can be anti-Castro, but if that automatically makes you pro-Batista at a time that Castro's about to take over, you've obviously got a problem on your hands. And what we needed was a diplomat who was skilled at being neutral, and who did not let himself get identified as openly one way or the other, as both those fellows had.

Q: Who made the decision to cut off the arms shipments to Batista? The one that was made while you were away?

RUBOTTOM: I think that recommendation undoubtedly started somewhere in my bureau. I wouldn't want to say which person was responsible for it. We had a munitions section in the embassy. They would have had to concur in it. And then, of course, the decision would have had to be finally approved by the Under-Secretary and the Secretary of State himself. I talked to Bill Snow, my deputy, when I got back, and he described the afternoon that he went up and talked to Secretary Dulles about this, and Secretary Dulles really approved it, so I don't know that there's much point in saying that somebody else did it. I think you'd have to say the Secretary did it.

Q: Just as he approved the appointment of Smith.

RUBOTTOM: That's right.

Q: In his memoirs, President Eisenhower wrote that in the final days of 1958, the CIA suggested that a Castro victory might not be in the best interests of the United States, and that he, Eisenhower, was provoked that this conclusion hadn't been reached earlier. Was his complaint justified?

RUBOTTOM: Well, perhaps it's justified, yes. I'm very sympathetic to the President. I saw the draft of that book before it was published, and I know there was a lot of soul-searching that went into that part of it. I got a few ideas that were accepted and some that weren't, as a matter of fact, in exchanges with his son, John, who was the principal editor of the book.

Now, I think that long before the end of 1958, there were some very strong questions—in my mind at least—about Castro. In fact, I can't believe that the CIA itself didn't have quite a number of those questions, because I was talking to some CIA people regularly. I think what they were always hoping was that Batista would have a *bona fide* election and he would step aside [if he lost], or failing that, that Batista would see the handwriting on the wall and step out in time for a junta to take over, a junta that would be made up of respected people who could preside over elections and could sidetrack Castro. And I think the regrettable thing was that Batista simply never would accept this kind of advice, and he stayed on until it was too late for anything to be done. By this time, of course, Castro took over in sole power rather than having either to work with a junta or to be a force that a junta without Castro would have to reckon with.

Q: President Eisenhower suggests in his book that the only

This photograph of President Dwight D. Eisenhower is inscribed, "For Ambassador Roy R. Rubottom, Jr., with best wishes and warm regards for a distinguished American—from his friend, Dwight D. Eisenhower."

hope at the end of 1958 seemed to be a non–dictatorial third force. Was he referring to the possibility of a junta?

RUBOTTOM: Yes, I think so.

Q: Was there any real prospect of this?

RUBOTTOM: Well, I think there might have been, if it had been put together in time—if there had been a chance of this happening in the fall, even sixty or ninety days before Batista finally left the country on New Year's Eve of '58 or '59. This might have had a chance. But by staying on until the bitter end when the jig was up? It was too late.

Q: But you think in the fall, let's say three months earlier, it might possibly have succeeded?

RUBOTTOM: It might possibly have succeeded, and as you know, this has been printed in public so there's no secret about it—former Ambassador and Assistant Secretary of State William Pawley went down to Cuba. [Son of a wealthy businessman in Cuba, Pawley grew up in Cuba and later went back as president of the *Nacional Cubana de Aviacion* Curtiss; subsequently he was Ambassador to Cuba.] He actually made two trips trying to talk Batista into stepping aside earlier, and he had the gall to state later in a published article of some kind—I think it was Fulton Lewis [well-known radio and television broadcaster in the 1930s and 1940s] or somebody like that who wrote it—that he probably would have succeeded if the State Department had permitted him to state that he came there with the authority of the President.

Well, I remember going to the CIA and talking about this with Allen Dulles, who was then head of the CIA, present. I remember Mr. Pawley sitting right there with me and the opposite number (to me) from the CIA, and we talked about this journey that he was going to make down there. Obviously, if you're going to send a man to represent the President, you use the Ambassador; you don't use a man of this kind. Why was Mr. Pawley suggesting himself? And he did suggest himself for this role.

Q: He suggested himself.

RUBOTTOM: Yes. It was because he'd been in business in Cuba for many, many years, and had actually known Batista from the time that he came in as sergeant, working as receptionist and secretary for Machado, 1934. He'd known

Rubottom was often called on to answer questions about U.S. policy.

him well, and he knew also that Batista knew the role that Pawley played in the United States and that he had been a high official in the State Department as well as Ambassador in two countries: Peru and Brazil.

So he didn't have to go down there with any written credentials, you know. A man on a CIA mission of that kind doesn't show an exequatur [patent which a head of state issues to a foreign consul which guarantees the consul's rights and privileges of the office] or carry with him a diploma showing that he is coming from the President. He goes in because he knows this person and this person knows he can speak with authority. I just think he was ineffective. And I knew it was a tough job. I don't criticize Mr. Pawley for not succeeding, so much as I do for trying to pass the buck to somebody else for his lack of success.

Q: He suggested himself for this and Allen Dulles picked up the suggestion?

RUBOTTOM: Yes. I'm sure he was feeding information all the time into the CIA from his own trips to Cuba. He had big business interests . . . in Cuba.

Q: Did President Eisenhower approve his missions down there?

RUBOTTOM: I honestly don't know whether the President knew that he was going down there or not. It's quite possible that the President did not know it. I think the likelihood is that he did, though, because I know Mr. Pawley, and Mr. Pawley was not going to do anything like that without the President's knowing it. I'm not even sure that Mr. Pawley would have succeeded in getting himself named for that mission if he hadn't gone to see the President, because his shortcomings, and he had his share of them (we all are human), are pretty well known around Washington, including to the CIA.

Q: President Eisenhower mentions in his memoirs that after the CIA report submitted toward the end of 1958, one of his advisors suggested that the U.S. should now back Batista as the lesser of the two evils. Can you throw any light on that?

RUBOTTOM: This is one of the great anomalies, I think of diplomacy—how you use power to bear in some way that destroys its very usefulness, by overcoming let's say the non-intervention doctrine and other things of this kind. I don't think there's anything much the United States could have done without incurring ill to an unacceptable degree all over Latin America, as well as at home, if in late 1958 we had somehow tried to give this kind of backing to Batista. If someone did suggest that to him, I think he was dead right in rejecting it.

Q: Now, when Castro came to the United States in April of 1959, he was invited by the American Society of Newspaper Editors to talk to their convention. Did that upset the State Department?

RUBOTTOM: It upset the State Department very much, especially me. Yes, sir, it certainly did. I learned about it when I read in the paper that this invitation had been issued, and that he had accepted it, and it was issued by a committee of three people representing the editors, one of whom was my very good friend Jules Dubois . . . of the *Chicago Tribune*. [Others included} the editor of the *Washington Daily News*, John O'Rourke, and the editor of a New Orleans paper, either the *Times Picayune* or *Item*,

George Healy, who was chairman of the committee. This put us in a terrible spot, for at least a couple of reasons.

Our policy after Castro took over had to go through about three phases. The first phase was that of probing and testing to find out just who he was and what kind of

In April 1959, Fidel Castro visited the United States at the invitation of the American Society of Newspaper Editors. President Eisenhower declined to meet with him, and sent Rubottom in his stead.

person he was. He was virtually unknown, and he had two sets of advisors around him, those who were pro-Communist or Communist and those who were anti-Communist but who had fought with him in the underground, and he had some very good people in that second group. So there had to be a good deal of testing to find out whether they were going to gain the upper hand or whether the others were going to gain the upper hand, as they eventually did.

Well, by inviting him to the United States, we were making a declaratory judgment on him as a public—I say we, I'm talking about the United States public at large, that he was a fit person for an invitation, more than just a subject for news, and that he had sort of proven himself, and that he could come and cash in his hero's chips, so to speak, in this country, after having been built up by Herbert Matthews. Jules Dubois had built him up and many others. This was one problem.

Now the bigger problem was what would he say or do after he got here that would make it far more difficult to deal with him? And he did exactly that. I mean, he used this platform, first in Washington and later in New York and Harvard and Princeton and Houston . . . as a platform to just give outright lies to direct questions, which were totally misleading to the public and which for all practical purposes ended the probing and testing in the public mind, but didn't do anything but just make the mask over his face harder to penetrate as far as we [in the State Department] were concerned.

They asked him if he was going to have elections, and he said, "Yes." He promised to have elections, I think within a year. They asked him if he was a Communist and he said, "No." They asked him if Cuba would remain a member of the OAS, and he said, "Yes." They asked him if Cuba would desist in trying to export its style of revolution—I think there'd already been one or two minor incursions from the island—and he said that they would desist, that they would not try to export it.

Oh yes, and the big question, they asked him if he would treat American investment in Cuba, which was over a billion dollars, fairly, and he said yes, that they needed it.

Now I ask you, what kind of platform could a man have to better serve his interests than this—no matter what his intentions were deep down?

But you see, there really is a third factor, and this had involved the reputation of the State Department and, to some extent, my own reputation at the State Department, down through the years since this occurred. It's generally not believed by the public that the State Department didn't have something to do with this visit. There's nothing further from the truth. We didn't. We deplored it. To this day I think it was one of the worst problems that we had to deal with.

Q: Did you make any effort to have the invitation withdrawn?

RUBOTTOM: No. No, he'd already accepted it. And this is the kind of delicacy that you get involved in [as a diplomat]. I was talking about Smith a while ago, and he came out with a perfectly good statement deploring what happened to those ladies in Santiago, and nearly got kicked out of the country, and it scared him to death, and he wouldn't open his mouth after that. Well, after outsiders, newspapermen admittedly, but outsiders from the government, had invited Castro, it would have put the government in the most baleful light to have said, "Sorry, we won't receive him."

Q: Well, the President mentions in his memoirs that he himself asked if we couldn't refuse a visa.

RUBOTTOM: Well, I think that was a rhetorical question.

Q: Do you think we could have done more during this period to woo Castro?

RUBOTTOM: Well, I don't know what more we could have done, frankly. I will admit my own bias. I've already indicated it. But I had doubts about him because of the destructive approach he took to changing things in his country. But I talked to Castro when he was in Washington and I talked to Castro when he was in Buenos Aires about two months later. There was an economic meeting down there that he attended, and he asked to see me alone. I saw him alone in the Hotel Alfonso Treci, and he wasn't alone. He had his economic minister with him. We had a fairly good discussion. But I don't mean to say that my role in this would have been decisive. Far from it. We were doing everything we could to try to work with their ambassador in Washington. They sent a very skilled and trained diplomat who found, after he took the job, that he couldn't get to Castro at all. Castro never gave him a hearing. He went down one time and spent six weeks and never got to see Castro, at a time when we were trying to discuss some of the problems involving our investments there.

One of the most overt moves to woo Castro that was made was the assignment of Phil Bonsel as the Ambassador there. Smith came home. It was pretty obvious that he wasn't the man to try to deal with Castro.

Now, Phil Bonsal is well known all over Latin America as a man who speaks Spanish about as perfectly as any U.S. diplomat. He is a fairly well-known liberal, and in trying to do his role with Castro he incurred the ill will of a number of our other ambassadors, particularly political ambassadors who tried to do him in later and probably succeeded, to some extent, in shortening his career. But he, too, was unsuccessful [in Cuba].

We had as good a man, I think, in the person of Bonsal,

as we could have sent. I don't know what we could have done, frankly. Castro was so busy trying to consolidate his own position and trying to make up his mind which one of his advisors he was going to listen to—or assuming the worst, that he was always a Communist, in allowing a certain minimum time to pass before he announced his true colors. I don't think that assumption is valid but some might assume it. I think it became fairly clear what Castro was in late May or early June, when he came down on the side of the extreme Agrarian Reform Act. There was a softer version of that which he could have accepted, that would have permitted private farms to continue operating, and private enterprise to function in this whole sector of their economy. Instead, he came down on the extreme side, favoring an agrarian reform act of the most outrageous kind.

Q: Would you regard that as a turning point? Did our approach to Castro or attitude toward him change after that point?

RUBOTTOM: I would say that we began to recognize then that we were dealing with a force that, irrespective of its ideological base—that is, Communist or not, was so anti-U.S. that we were going to have a serious problem on our hands. Yes, by June or July of 1959, I think we knew this. If you could say that the period of probing and testing ended at that time, then we entered into the second phase, which was somehow or other to unmask Castro for what he really was.

There were a number of things that happened in the summer of 1959 that put Castro clearly over into the Communist side—the Agrarian Reform Act I've already referred to. The seeking of several of his non-Communist advisors or their decision to leave the administration. A couple of his non-Communist lieutenants—one of them was arrested and one of them disappeared without much explanation on a small plane flight going over to Camaguay, or somewhere in central Cuba.

By this time, Secretary Mann [Thomas Mann] and I began to look ahead to what was going to be a number one problem the following year, and that was the sugar legislation. This had to come up for renewal, and we began to take a pretty firm position that the President ought to have the authority, the discretionary authority, to cancel quotas at any time. We had an awful time getting this through the Congress, and we faced the opposition of several influential people who were playing an effective role, decidedly pro-Castro people. But finally the administration's desires in this respect to give the President authority were included in the legislation. It was passed after an all-night session in the summer of 1960, late June or early July, and then about three or four days later, the President canceled the sugar quota. And this was the beginning of what you might call the open confrontation with the Castro regime.

Q: What steps did we take in Phase 2 toward unmasking Castro?

RUBOTTOM: Well, I think, for one thing, we saw to it that he was well publicized—we tried to do this through the public media and through information media and through CIA channels and everything else, the extent to which Castro was trying to export his revolution—the way he was attempting through subversion and penetration, if not outright invasion, to influence the outcome of political events in other countries, notably Costa Rica, Panama, Haiti, the Dominican Republic, and Venezuela. I guess there wasn't anything more serious than the effort that Castro made to dislodge the elected regime, and finally I think he began to pull back to some extent from this kind of open statement.

Q: Now, when the President made his trip to Latin America in early 1960, was there a lot of discussion with the heads of other government about Castro?

RUBOTTOM: I don't think this was a principal subject of discussion. Of course, it came up. I wasn't always present at the time the President talked to the other Presidents. I was not the interpreter, and I was sometimes with Secretary Herter or with Dr. Milton Eisenhower, or maybe they would go to the President. We actually divided up, for example in Argentina, and went in two different directions for a day and a half. But I participated in the drafting of all the speeches that the President made. Dr. Eisenhower and I did that. And of course I was privy to the messages that were sent and all the reports that came back. I think we were more interested in talking about economic development and what we could do to help Latin America than we were in talking about the negative problem of the threat of Castro.

Q: So we weren't really as a priority item trying to line up opposition to him, then?

RUBOTTOM: No, I wouldn't say that we were.

Q: Shortly after the President came back, I believe in March 1960, the CIA began organizing the training of Cuban exiles. Where did that policy originate?

RUBOTTOM: Well, that policy originated in the State Department and with the CIA. I had something to do with it. As I told you, I met all the time with my opposite number in the CIA. I became convinced, by the fall of 1959, that it was not going to be possible to work with Castro, and I began to see it specifically as a threat to our country, because of the Communist penetration there, and I approached

Secretary Murphy [Assistant Secretary for Near Eastern and South Asian Affairs, Richard W. Murphy] one day and asked if I could meet with him and Allen Dulles after one of their regular Wednesday or Thursday luncheons. The top people in the intelligence community met regularly. And he said I could, and I told him that I had concluded, on the basis of all that I had been able to see, that the Castro regime was totally inimical to the best interests of the United States, and that it behooved us to try to support the anti-Castro elements.

They thought it over, and I got a green light to go ahead and work on a memorandum, and I prepared a memorandum which had . . . in it the fact that Cuba might become a threat to the United States because of the possible implantation of Soviet missiles. This was written early in January or February 1960. And the President approved the policy in March of 1960, and it then became the responsibility of the CIA to execute this.

I went to Argentina as ambassador in September, so I was away from the United States and knew nothing about the way this thing was being carried out. I would probably have had some sense of the way it was being done.

As you know, the effort aborted, for quite a number of reasons. I've always felt that one of the reasons was the undue publicity that it was given in advance, so that everything that was being done was being published in the newspapers in Miami and New York almost at the time it was being done. I could see that from as far away as Buenos Aires, where I was.

One might properly inquire, how could an officer in the State Department who espoused the basic principle of the American republics, and one that the United States had adopted long since—that of non-intervention—make such a recommendation to his government?

Well, I have figured out along these lines, and I personally think it is a defensible rationale and that it's not just a rationalization. It wasn't accidental that the Rio Treaty was enacted in the summer of 1947, prior to the OAS charter in the spring of 1948. The Rio Treaty was the one that established the whole doctrine of collective security, and as you know, this antedated the NATO treaty by several months. It had our most distinguished Senators and General Marshall present at the time of its negotiation, and I feel that in order for a country to formally enter into—and prior to this time we had not formally undertaken by treaty—I guess we had, but we had not put it certainly into any kind of an OAS charter—the question of non-intervention—I think one has to be sure that his security is going to be upheld. One cannot commit himself not to intervene if he feels that his security is threatened. Well, our security had been assured, we thought, by the Rio Treaty.

The doctrine, simply stated, is that an attack against one is an attack against all. We had ample evidence of outright intervention and actual attacks against several of the other American republics by Castro. We had the prospect of the sale of Soviet arms, because it was becoming increasingly evident that Cuba was going toward Communism, and as I told you, we expressed in our rationale the fear that we might have missiles planted that could be aimed at the United States. This was more than two years earlier than the actual Cuban missile crisis. If it weren't in the memorandum I wouldn't of course say this, but I just want to assure you that it's not a case of hindsight.

So we tried, all through 1959, at the Santiago meeting of foreign ministers and through two meetings of foreign ministers in the summer of 1960 at San Jose, Costa Rica, one of them involving the Dominican Republic, which we dealt with first—which was the rightist kind of dictatorship—and the other one involving Cuba, which we dealt with secondly, which was the leftist kind of dictatorship, and they're both threats to the hemisphere.

Now, unfortunately we had to deal fairly softly with the Cubans because, for reasons which I shan't try to detail here, we found a soft attitude on the part of Latin-Americans. And had Secretary Dulles still been alive, I think he would have been terribly disillusioned—he who was the author of the Caracas Resolution in 1954, which particularized on the threat of Communism by word. Because heretofore and in the Rio Treaty we'd dealt only with an enemy I think with aggressive intentions or something to that effect without particularizing it, because at that time in 1948 I guess we were more concerned with Fascist type dictatorships than we were with Communist type dictatorships.

But at any rate, the Latin-Americans, in one negotiation after another for a period of two years, had shown themselves simply unwilling to face up to this security threat, and to do the thing jointly with the United States that would have enabled us to protect ourselves from Castro.

So this is the primary reason that I felt that the security of the United States ultimately had to come first, because the one treaty commitment, that of non-intervention, was to a large extent negated by the other treaty commitment of collective security which they were unwilling to commit themselves to do anything about.

Now, so much for the rationale. I had already said that I had gone to Argentina by the 1st of September, 1960. I know nothing about the details with which this enterprise was mounted. Obviously the United States was going to try to work through the anti-Castro Cubans and the exiles. But as I say, a problem obviously appeared in the extent to which this was publicized by the newspapers and the magazines. I remember being shocked as I read about it in Argentina.

Then, of course, there was the problem of the transition in government from Eisenhower to Kennedy, and this in itself might have been a problem that should have caused the whole thing to be called off. But when you come to the actual showdown, and I'm about to finish on this point, there were four alternatives that President Kennedy could have chosen among. He could have called off the planned invasion. He could have postponed it. He could have given it the support that it required in order to be successful—and I can assure you that President Eisenhower would never have backed anything like that if he hadn't intended to carry it through and see it through, because you take all the onus of intervention without accomplishing what it purports to do. Or last, doing what we did do, let the thing get started and withhold the support to make it succeed. This was the worst of all four alternatives, and it was a tragedy.

Now, to President Kennedy's credit, I'll have to say that on April 21st, four days after the invasion started on the 17th, he went before the press and assumed the full responsibility for it. And this pretty well cut off criticism. Criticism didn't really begin to come until after he'd been assassinated. But I think it's very important that some of these things eventually get into the record.

Q: Did you ever discuss this with President Eisenhower?

RUBOTTOM: No. No, I never did discuss it with President Eisenhower.

Q: Your conversations on it were with Allen Dulles and—

RUBOTTOM: Robert Murphy, and to some extent with the members of the Inter-American Advisory Committee, which was appointed in 1958, I believe, by Secretary Dulles, which consisted of Charles Meyer, now Assistant Secretary, then with Sears Roebuck, former ambassador Walter Donnelly, Dana Munro who'd been a teacher at Princeton after years in the government way back in the early days of the 1920s and 1930s, and Milton Eisenhower, who was then president of the International Institute for Education.

Q: Kenneth Holland?

RUBOTTOM: Kenneth Holland, and Jack Knight. I believe there were six members. Jack was a member of the AFL-CIO, head of the Oil Workers Union. They were aware of this, and this includes Milton, and I don't doubt that Milton and his brother probably talked about it to some extent. But as I say, the details of something like this quite properly do not involve the State Department personnel, even though they may have been involved in a policy determination to give support. Now, this support can be any of several kinds, to the anti-Castro Cubans.

Q: Was there any real opposition to this general policy among those with whom you discussed it?

RUBOTTOM: If there was, I never did hear of it. I would guess that, by the late fall and winter of 1960 and 1961, I'm sure that you could probably drive a truck between the two sides, in Washington, as to whether it should or should not be done. I just can't believe all the publicity that was attendant to it, with the *New York Times* and *Life Magazine* and *Time* and other [publications] writing about it all the time—and most of them against it, of course. I think the very fact that it became public was enough [reason] to call it off. Something of this kind requires almost full cover— that is, full covertness—to be successful. And then the other point that I made earlier: you've got to be prepared to give it the backing to make it succeed, or you don't accept the onus of intervening anyway, which we did in this case.

Q: But the planning was fairly closely held within government, wasn't it?

RUBOTTOM: I'm sure it was. I didn't know anything about it. I was an ambassador in Argentina.

Q: What was the reaction of the Argentines when you put the question to them? You said you sounded them out once or twice.

RUBOTTOM: Yes, I think they were fully prepared for it and fully expected it to succeed.

Q: And would have gone along with it?

RUBOTTOM: And would have gone along. There might have been a mild editorial tap on the wrist or two here and there by certain newspapers in Argentina, but the bulk of the newspapers would have gone along with it and I think the government would have gone along with it.

Q: Were there any people with whom you discussed it who notably agreed with it? Very strongly seconded it?

RUBOTTOM: Well, I didn't discuss it with very many people. I think you can understand why. I just couldn't. By this time, my own skin was beginning to be pretty sensitive to what I was taking in public by those who were accusing me of being pro-Castro. This is the odd thing about all this, you know. Nathaniel Wild's book *Red Star Over Cuba*, just to cite one—Earl E.T. Smith's book, came along a little bit later—but these books had me painted, you know, as a

Castro-lover. I guess if I had been like Mr. Pawley, and I don't see any point in mincing words here, as opportunistic as he was, I would have somehow or other tried to be like a chameleon, and take on the coloration of whatever particular policy seemed to be popular at the time. But I never did play my cards that way. (I might say here again in parenthesis about my own personality and my own philosophy—I am a person who comes fairly close to being an iconoclast. I'm an individualist, and I think labels disturb me, and I don't think many of them fit me. I get very upset in the Dallas community, reading the newspapers trying to call everybody either a liberal or a conservative. I know that I'm extremely liberal on some questions, and I know that I'm extremely conservative on certain others and I think most people are like that. It's very hard to find one who can be categorized a hundred percent one way or the other—that is, as liberal or conservative.)

I did my best to uphold the ideals to which we were committed, but I feel that this obligation falls with equal weight on the other partners to any kind of commitment, and when the other side refuses to uphold his part of the bargain, I don't think that we are then bound to carry out to the last letter something that—going back to this question of non-intervention—[something that puts] our own security at stake—and when I find that there's utter weakness on the part of our Latin-American neighbors in upholding their commitments under the Rio Treaty, as far as the collective security is concerned, or even frowning hard on Castro. Mind you, we couldn't even mention Castro by name finally in the document that came out of the San Jose Conference in 1960. And this was a year and eight months after he'd been in power, and he'd shown his colors by that time. He hadn't called himself a Communist, but I think it was in July, just before that meeting, that—who was it, Mikoyan, wasn't it? [Anastas Hovhannesi Mikoyan, First

Deputy Premier of the Soviet Union]—who visited and made the statement that said, in effect, that it was a conditional threat toward the United States and the rest of Latin America. So there's no reason why they should have been so mushy-mouthed about the Cuban threat. It was pretty real by then.

Q: Were there any countries or any Latin-American leaders in particular who were a problem as being very soft on Castro?

RUBOTTOM: Yes, and this will be surprising. Probably one of the softest ones was Venezuela. . . . In fact, in 1959, at the Santiago meeting of foreign ministers, Secretary Herter [U.S. Secretary of State who followed John Foster Dulles] was in the delegate's chair and I was sitting right behind him, and next to us was Venezuela's foreign Minister and one or two others in their delegation. We sat there for a week together, day after day, and the Venezuelan, who was a rather emotional type, reacted so strongly to the effort by somebody—I don't think it was Secretary Herter, but somebody else referred to the Caracas Declaration of 1954, which was the extension of the Rio Treaty that I referred to a moment ago, specifically naming Communism as a threat that would require joint action in the hemisphere. And when this mention of the Caracas Declaration happened, here we are now in 1959, and the Pérez Jiménez government had been overthrown about a year and a half by this time and I think Betancourt had been elected president by then—and Betancourt had always been accused of being a Communist, and then after he became president, the Communists were among the greatest threats to him.

Anyway, the foreign minister gets up and, in an emotion-packed voice, says, "I will consider it an insult to my country if any delegate again mentions the capital of my own country in connection with the declaration of 1954, because that declaration came at a time when the OAS meeting that occurred was sponsored by the arch-dictatorship of the hemisphere, Pérez Jiménez."

So here you have a country threatened itself by Communism, unwilling even to acknowledge that there was such a declaration, let alone adhere to it, even though its own capital had its name on it, because it was done at a time when the Pérez Jiménez dictatorship was in control of the government.

Q: Your suggestion to Allen Dulles and Murphy, your original suggestion was influenced by all these developments, but was there any particular thing that prompted it? Any specific action?

RUBOTTOM: No. I can be quite clear in saying that we went through a careful period of probing and testing. We set one of the best prepared ambassadors we had, one who did everything he could to work with Castro. We had a good ambassador from Cuba in Washington who was totally ineffective and finally admitted that he couldn't do anything. Secretary Herter and I had talked to Raul Roa, who was the foreign minister of Cuba, down in Santiago, as we had talked to the other foreign ministers. I'd had him down from the U.N., Foreign Minister Roa, to talk to him, to see what we could do. By this time the hammering against our investments was beginning to increase, and one by one they were being taken over, so by the fall of 1959, I simply saw a concatenation of events, rather than any single event, that led me to make that recommendation.

Q: Roa was rather easy to talk to, wasn't he?

RUBOTTOM: Yes, he was approachable. He was a very

volatile man with a hot temper and extremely Latin in his gesticulations and so on, but yes, he was easy to talk to.

Q: Did you feel, in your talks with Roa, that you were making any progress?

RUBOTTOM: No. Frankly, any more than when I talked to Castro, and I talked to him for at least 35, 40 minutes I guess, maybe an hour, down in Buenos Aires.

Q: What do you recall of that particular meeting? You say this was requested by Castro.

RUBOTTOM: Yes. What I did was to say that I was delighted to see him again—now, mind you, this was in May of 1958. He'd been in office about five months. And I told him that we were working hard with his ambassadors in Washington—he had two, one to the United States and one to the OAS—and that we had a number of problems that we felt needed urgent attention, and that we knew that his country had severe economic problems. We had only a short time before we authorized a second draw-down of $40 million under the International Monetary Fund to help them out. I mean, we had given our vote in favor of it. And that we felt that this could only go on for a short time before there would have to be steps taken to try to increase the flow of investment and other capital, including the Inter-American Bank, which was beginning to get organized at that time, and its corporation and chartering was just around the corner—and could we get down to brass tacks, detailed negotiations on these problems? And he gave me every assurance that we could, and I wrote a memorandum when we got through, in which I stated all this, and I think I put at the end, "His ability, let alone his desire, to carry through on this commitment, is subject entirely to question." I had no certainty at all of his desire, let alone his ability, to carry out anything he said.

Q: You gauged this just from his attitude in his talk?

RUBOTTOM: Yes.

Q: I believe President Eisenhower then suggested to the State Department that a front be organized among the Cuban exiles, which the U.S. would then recognize. Do you have any idea whatever happened to that suggestion?

RUBOTTOM: Was this put in his book? This wasn't made public.

Q: That's right, it was in his book.

RUBOTTOM: Well, of course the book was published after the Bay of Pigs. Inherent in this plan that the CIA was working on, I am confident, was the installation of some kind of a government, you see. If the internal rebellion was not much to overthrow him immediately, you could have at least had a part of the island which would have been in the hands of this rebellious group that could have been recognized and could have gotten aid. A state of belligerence could have been recognized . . . Undoubtedly, this was what they had in mind.

Q: Of course, I imagine it would have been quite difficult to get the Cuban exiles to agree on leadership.

RUBOTTOM: Yes, I would guess that this was just about as difficult as trying to deal with Castro, and that's one of the tragedies of Cuba.

Q: Did you have much contact with the exile groups?

RUBOTTOM: No. No.

Q: The President also mentions in his book that in 1960, emergency plans for Cuba were kept ready; that these included blockades, military action, and joint action with Latin-American countries. Were there a number of contingency plans in the period before you went to Argentina?

RUBOTTOM: I wasn't aware of any of these. Of course, the Inter-American Defense Board had certain contingency plans. This was an agency that operated rather tenuously on its own, without even a dotted line relationship, or no more than that, to the OAS, because the OAS political council never would—in the Inter-American conferences which we used to have in those days—never would actually recognize them. They were always afraid to give any power to the military arm of this OAS group. But I am sure that, looking forward to what eventually became the Bay of Pigs, there had to be some kind of contingency planning. Suppose the Russians had tried to come in and do something? Suppose they'd gotten in clandestinely? There's just no telling. We had to be prepared for all kinds of things like that, and of course, the Cubans had given ample demonstration of certain kinds of crass courage, in their attempts to invade and subvert other countries around. Of course they couldn't subvert us very well, but . . .

Q: Ambassador Rubottom, would you discuss the Dominican Republic?

RUBOTTOM: The Dominican Republic always was held up as the archetype of repressive dictatorship, military dictatorship. It was the oldest in the hemisphere. There had been others—Honduras and Nicaragua, [for example]. By this time, of course, Somoza was dead, and the Honduran dictator had been replaced, and Pérez Jiménez had been overthrown. So I think this emboldened the editorial writers of Latin America, as well as the people in governments of Latin America who were extremely anti-dictator, to take more and more extreme positions, some of which were critical of the United States for its "support of dictatorships."

I don't suppose I ever faced a press conference in all my many trips around Latin America during the time that I was Assistant Secretary, or even when I was Ambassador in Argentina, that I didn't have someone ask me this question. They always loaded it by imputing to the United States support of dictatorships, and I had to start off by knocking this down—[saying] that we didn't support dictatorships at all. We tried to maintain relationships with them, and to the extent that those relations were amenable, we might even be able to influence them toward some democratic stance. Of course, Batista was a part of this also, and you might say that Batista and Trujillo became the symbols, literally hated all over the hemisphere. And of course there was great editorial comment and magazine comment in the United States about our so-called support.

Well, Batista took it on the lam and Castro took over, so this left Trujillo. Trujillo was a problem. He had become totally corrupt, totally amoral, had absolutely no support whatsoever, though with very, very little open opposition at home. It was not until, I guess, sometime in 1960 that the opposition became strong enough to make the move that they finally did when they assassinated him.

Now, this may have been brought on, in part, by the fact that Trujillo actually tried to assassinate Betancourt [Rómulo Ernesto Betancourt Bello, president of Venezuela from 1945 to 1948 and again from 1959 to 1964]. You may recall that the Betancourt car went by the place where there was an explosion, and he barely escaped with his life. He was injured and I think one of the people in the car was killed. Well, this just increased the opposition to Trujillo all over Latin America. And this just intensified our problem of trying to deal with Castro. As far as we were concerned, we had a rightist dictator and a leftist dictator, and they're both bad, and we didn't try to distinguish between them. But we had to deal with the Trujillo problem primarily because of our Latin-American friends, in the first of the two back-to-back conferences that were held in Costa Rica in 1960—and we came down for the first time in the history of the O.A.S. with an outright sanction of a country. We sanctioned the trade and finance of the Dominican Republic at that foreign ministers' meeting. Then, of course, we had the meeting to deal with the Castro problem, and we couldn't even get Castro mentioned by name in the declaration.

So the answer is yes, he [Trujillo] was very much of a problem. Of course, he was eliminated by assassination [on May 30, 1961].

Q: We eventually came to the point of breaking relations with the Dominican Republic?

RUBOTTOM: Yes. This was done. This was one of the sanctions, as I recall, that was voted in that August meeting.

Q: Our major concern, then, our major problem—that is, apart from wanting to help Latin America economically— our major problem during your time as Assistant Secretary was certainly Cuba, wasn't it?

RUBOTTOM: Yes. . . . And it *was* negative. It was a security threat of the first kind to the United States, and I just can't imagine, if President Kennedy had lived, what he would have eventually written, because I have the clear feeling—and this is important to get into the record—that his indecisiveness and the option that he did choose at the time of the Bay of Pigs in 1961 led directly to the Cuban Missile Crisis in 1962. The Soviets miscalculated. I think it was beyond the Soviet understanding that we would not actually have gone ahead and made that support sufficient to succeed, and once we didn't do that, I think they said, "My gosh, we can probably move in there and do anything we want to."

Then he had a much more serious threat to deal with.

Q: Allen Dulles—President Eisenhower in his book again says that Allen Dulles told him in the summer of 1960, [in] July, that the Soviets might be preparing to establish short range missiles in Cuba. Was there any indication at that time?

RUBOTTOM: You couldn't fail to conclude that this would be one of the things they might do. Our paper that I told you about, that went to the President, which he signed in March 1960, said this, and the man who helped me draft that paper was my most direct liaison at the working level with all of the CIA. That was his principal work. So I'm not at all surprised that Allen Dulles would have said this in July of 1960.

Q: Who was the person with whom you worked in the CIA?

RUBOTTOM: Well, I never have mentioned his name. You mean my opposite number in the CIA?

Q: Yes.

RUBOTTOM: I never have mentioned his name to anybody. Maybe it's come out somewhere. I'll mention it and then I'll decide later whether I want to cut it out: his name is J. C. King. But I'd prefer not to mention my assistant in the State Department who helped me draft this paper, who was dealing at a level below King all the time, because he's still on active duty in the State Department.

Q: And you believe there's still some feeling in the State Department . . .

RUBOTTOM: I think so. I don't think we have anything to be ashamed of, myself. I'm rather proud of it, and one of these days I'd like to get it out in the open, because I have been unfairly accused so many times by people who really did not know what we were trying to do and how complex the task was, that I think in fairness to myself and my family and to what I attempted to do, it needs to be brought out.

Q: Just one or two wind-up questions. To what extent was Dr. Milton Eisenhower an influence on Latin-American policy after the death of Secretary Dulles?

RUBOTTOM: I think it remained steady at a very high level. I think it was perhaps diluted, to some extent, by virtue of his being on the Inter-American Advisory Council, which incidentally was another effort on our part to bring in these people of distinction and show that Latin America rated high in the minds of the President and the Secretary of State, and was not just at the bottom of the list of priorities.

Q: What were the relations between Dr. Eisenhower and Secretary Dulles?

RUBOTTOM: I would say they were good. They were probably not close or even warm, but they were good. Mr. Dulles was a difficult person to get close to, although I felt that I had his ear and had his respect and I admired the man. I think some of this was his rather puritanical up-bringing. His father, I believe, was a clergyman, and he [John Foster Dulles] was a very strong-willed, self-disciplined man who'd studied and worked hard all of his life, and had been successful. And of course [Dulles had a] Wall Street lawyer background before he went into diplomacy late in life. Milton Eisenhower, by contrast, had always been an academician, so they had trod different paths. I think they had a mutual respect for each other. I [never saw] any problem between them.

CHAPTER 10

A Diplomatic Tour of South America 1958

Dick Rubottom had close dealings with Richard Nixon, and in recalling those experiences, he says, "Like most Americans, my first significant encounter with Nixon was on the TV screens. This was in 1952. Presidential nominee Dwight Eisenhower had to choose a Vice-Presidential candidate to run on the Republican ticket in the November election."

Rubottom goes on, "Nixon was already well-known to many Americans. Elected to the House of Representatives from California in 1946 after defeating the well-known Jerry Voorhis, Nixon quickly gained national attention. According to *The Contender*, Irwin F. Gellman's biography of Nixon, Nixon served in the Navy during World War II. He was not backed by wealthy patrons, but rather by staunch anti-New Deal businessmen, bankers, and growers. He earned his victory by tireless campaigning, spirited speeches, and clear conservative ideology, as well as thanks to his opponent's ineptitude."

Rubottom observes that, once in Congress, Nixon

worked hard. "He championed the anti-union Taft-Hartley Act and bucked his party's isolationists to back the Marshall Plan. His lead role in the House Un-American Activities Committee's interrogation of Alger Hiss quickly gained him stature—especially when Hiss was jailed for denying he had passed documents to Whitaker Chambers."

Triumphant, popular and ambitious, Nixon then defeated the well-known Helen Gahagan Douglas in a rambunctious, widely publicized race for the U.S. Senate in 1950, and Rubottom recalls that Nixon was thus poised, at age 30, when General Eisenhower beckoned, to become the first Republican Vice-President in twenty years.

Rubottom's personal acquaintance with Vice-President Nixon came during Nixon's second term in that office. "In 1956, I returned from my assignment in Madrid, and soon after, I was named Assistant Secretary of State for Inter-American Affairs, serving under Secretary John Foster Dulles, and, after Dulles' death, Secretary Christian Herter."

He goes on, "Right away I learned one of the informal, unpublicized guidelines of State Department assignments, and that is: Vice-Presidents are harder to deal with than Presidents, so be careful. One of my colleagues, the Assistant Secretary of State for African Affairs, had accompanied Vice-President Nixon on a long trip and he reiterated that point. I was to learn later how true it was."

In an effort to be fair, Rubottom adds that Vice-Presidents are not usually as well-acquainted with foreign relations problems as they are with domestic problems.

In any case, Rubottom's acquaintance with Nixon was to become more pronounced. In 1958, as Assistant Secretary for Inter-American Affairs, Rubottom was asked to accompany the Vice-President on a trip to South America. He recalls that the Eisenhower Administration at that time was in a defensive position about its policy in Latin America.

"It was sometimes asserted that the Eisenhower Administration was not interested in Latin America," he explains. "No matter what we said or did, no matter how many state visits we had from distinguished Latin-American leaders, we seemed vulnerable to that impression, or at least vulnerable enough to make us want to answer the charges."

So Nixon's diplomatic trip was devised as a way of showing the world, and especially certain countries in Latin America, that the United States was indeed interested in Latin-American affairs.

Dick Rubottom was central to the planning and execu-

Dick and Billy Ruth introduced Dick's mother, Jennie Eleanor Rubottom, to Vice-President Richard M. Nixon in August 1957.

tion of that trip, and consequently he found himself in the middle of historic events.

Dick notes that Vice-President Nixon had made an earlier trip through Central America, in 1953. "Nixon was known to be a vigorous, almost tireless individual, and well up to undertaking the physical challenge of a trip, during which we visited a number of countries. We believed the trip would display our unquestionable interest in Latin America. We were also interested in having a high-level delegation attend the inauguration of President Frondizi in Argentina, in late spring of 1958."

Dick recalls that the itinerary was complicated. "We had to decide which countries to visit or not visit, on what dates. Making these decisions required a great deal of time, so I designated the Office of Director of South American Affairs, and appointed a highly experienced diplomat named Maurice Birnbaum to that office. Birnbaum was to be the direct liaison with Vice-President Nixon's staff as we planned the trip. Maurice later became ambassador in Ecuador and then Venezuela.

"I might say here, parenthetically, that we knew then, and it probably hasn't changed, that the difficulty of dealing with Vice-Presidents on trips of this kind may reflect more on the office, with its built-in limitations, than it does the personality of the man. Or maybe it's both.

"But whatever the reasons, working with the Vice-President's staff is not simple. The staff has a way of being more demanding than the principal whom they serve, and naturally they're concerned about his security and about his getting the best possible press and all this sort of thing. So their views have to be respected, and besides, we had no one else to turn to. We knew we couldn't take up every detail with the Vice-President himself."

After Maurice Birnbaum began collaborating with the Nixon staff, it was decided that, for security reasons, the exact itinerary of the trip would not be made public until shortly before the group left the United States, even though the fact that he was going to South America had been announced.

"Early in the planning, we had to make a couple of decisions involving prominent countries," Dick goes on. "One such decision was whether or not the Vice-President should go to Chile. President Ibanez of Chile had, just shortly before, canceled an official trip to the United States on extremely short notice. This seemed like such a calculated slap that we felt it would be inappropriate for the Vice-President to visit Chile at that time.

"As for Venezuela, there had been a change of government only a few months earlier. The Pérez Jiménez dictatorship had been overthrown, and there was a five-man military junta government in authority. Thus we faced the question of whether to go to Venezuela and, if so, when. Things were still unstable there, and our interests and stakes in Venezuela were quite high. We didn't want to do anything that would light a match to a volatile situation."

However, as Rubottom and his team worked with Nixon's staff, it became clear that the Vice-President wanted to go to Venezuela. "With that, our recommendation became that he go there first," Rubottom says. "Knowing that there would be a critical security problem, knowing that there were interests adverse to the United States on the fringes of the junta, and knowing the volatility of the people after their having been under Pérez Jiménez for ten or eleven years, it just seemed best. Now that they were suddenly freed from that thumb of power, we in the State Department believed we should announce the trip at the last possible minute, and have Caracas be the Vice-President's first stop.

"However, we learned through his staff that the Vice-President would not adhere to our recommendations, and that he insisted that Caracas be the group's last stop. His reasoning, apparently, was partly political and public relations-oriented, in the sense that this would be a splendid take-off point for returning to the United States. I don't know how many thousands of Americans in those days were working in Venezuela, but there were billions of dollars invested there. The country was our relatively close neighbor, and some observers might have been considering the possibility of a Democratic constitutional government coming into authority there, after this long period of dictatorship in which no elected government had ever finished a term of office. This was true even before Pérez Jiménez."

In the end, not surprisingly, the Nixon view prevailed, and Caracas became the last stop on the trip. "Our recommendation was overruled," Dick says, and adds, "This is very significant if you stop to think about the way things unfolded later."

Pointing out that many of his recollections can be validated by at least one other person's judgment, Dick refers to Dr. Milton Eisenhower's book, *The Wine Is Bitter*, in which Dr. Eisenhower lays out opinions similar in tone and substance to Dick's own.

"We went to Uruguay first," Rubottom recalls. "We flew in a comfortable ten-passenger, twin-engine, propeller-driven plane (jets were not yet in use) that was assigned to the Chief of Naval Operations. The Vice-President and Mrs. Nixon had the main cabin. They always invited me to eat with them. The large press contingent filled a DC-4 commercial airplane, and usually landed before the Nixon plane.

"After a long overnight flight, our landing in Montevideo was uneventful. There was a sizeable reception group of Uruguayan government officials, American Embassy officials, and press waiting for us there. We went immediately to the hotel. It was early in the morning after an all-night trip. As we passed by the law school at the University of Montevideo, we saw perhaps a dozen young people standing on the curb. I believe they were throwing bills, or flyers. They didn't attract very much attention, although the forty or fifty press people who were traveling along behind the Vice-President naturally took note of them.

"When we got to the hotel, we began planning our activities for the afternoon. Then, just before we were to leave the hotel, we received word that the Vice-President was considering making a stop at the law school. Reportedly there were Communist and leftist-oriented students there who had expressed themselves against Nixon's visit only that morning."

As the senior State Department officials in the group, Dick and U.S. Ambassador to Uruguay Robert Woodward conferred on Nixon's desire to visit the law school. "Ambassador Woodward and I concluded that it would be wiser for the Vice-President not to go to the law school. Our recommendation, however, was either ignored or overruled. I'm not positive, in fact, that it was even brought to the Vice-President's attention. In any case, we did get in the cars and go to the law school, landing right in the lap of the activism. And I got into it myself."

Dick describes a chaotic but ultimately peaceful scene, in which students were eagerly asking questions of the visiting Americans. "The Vice-President had his own interpreter with him," he recalls, "and he was over in one room standing up on a desk and talking to some forty or fifty young people who were scattered around him. The translator was helping him. Ambassador Woodward, meanwhile, was in another room, while I was backed into a corner in a third room. Woodward and I didn't need interpreters, which was fortunate, because questions were being put to us as fast as we could answer them. In the end, we all left the campus just flushed with the euphoria of this relatively peaceful meeting."

Ultimately, though, the Americans came to believe that that scene was not entirely victorious, and today Dick reflects, "If it was a victory, it was a pyrrhic one. In my judgment, these events in Montevideo began the beat of drums that continued all the way up the line, for the rest of our trip. Bear in mind that Montevideo was our first stop, and we still had eight countries to visit."

The delegation spent another thirty-six hours in Montevideo before leaving for Argentina, where they would attend the inauguration of the new president of that country, Arturo Frondizi. While a law student at the University of Buenos Aires, Frondizi had demonstrated openly and repeatedly against the repressive government of Juan Perón. However, in his own subsequent presidential election campaign, as a representative of the Radical Civic Union, Frondizi supported democratization but also incorporated Peronists into the political process. Although this pragmatic philosophy caused a split in Frondizi's Radical Civic Union, whose leftist faction he represented, he nonetheless defeated the rightist candidate in the 1958 elections.

In support of these steps toward democratization, Vice-President Nixon and his U.S. entourage wanted to attend Frondizi's inauguration.

Dick recalls, "We left Argentina and had a short visit—only a few hours—in Paraguay. There were a number of questions asked about why the Vice-President visited this most disliked of all the dictatorships in Latin America, then ruled by Alfredo Stroessner Matiauda, military officer and dictator since 1954. However, Vice-President Nixon felt that a few hours there were justifiable. Earlier in the trip, the Vice-President had been trying to anticipate some of the questions he might be asked by the press. To me, the obvious question was, 'Why does the United States always seem to be in the position of supporting dictatorships—not only in Paraguay, but also, for example, Trujillo in the Dominican Republic?'

"In answer, Vice-President Nixon came up with a phrase that he used in one of his first press conferences on the trip. He said, and later repeated, 'The United States has a cool handclasp for dictatorships and a warm embrace for democratic governments.' This statement, needless to say, made Trujillo and a few others very angry, and it was used against us later, when we were trying to deal with Castro and Cuba. Of course, by that time Batista had become the archetype of the dictators and Castro was the symbol of the youth who were trying to overthrow them. Castro had not yet played his hand as a Communist."

After Argentina, the Vice-President and his entourage traveled to Bolivia, and then on to Peru. "By this time we were beginning to feel the heat from the Communists and extreme leftists, students, and others who wanted to try to embarrass the Vice-President on his trip," recalls Rubottom.

"In Peru, an incident took place at the University of San Marcos. This is rather important to me, because I remember we had a long discussion at the Hotel Bolivar in which our ambassador to Peru, Theodore Achilles, the Vice-President, and I engaged. There had been a threat of violence at San Marcos, and the Peruvian government had recommended that we not go. However, all of us agreed that we should go. In President Nixon's book, *The Six Crises*, for some reason he suggested that I advised him not to go. This was certainly not the case. Maurice Birnbaum and I have compared notes, and we are both quite certain that we took the position, along with Ambassador Achilles, that Mr. Nixon *should* go.

"So we went to San Marcos, where we had pebbles thrown at us, fairly good-sized pebbles, as a matter of fact. I remember one bouncing off my dark glasses when I was in an uncovered car. This is a rather personal memory for me, and one that was disputed by Nixon's book, where in that same few paragraphs about Peru, Nixon said that Ambassador Achilles and he went alone. In fact, Mr. Birnbaum and I were in the car right behind them, and we both clearly remember being there.

"Next we walked down to a very well-known and highly respected Catholic university, where we had a much different reception—although we still had to field surprisingly difficult questions.

"From there we traveled to Quito, Ecuador, and then to Bogotá. By the time we arrived in Colombia, American Embassy officials, in collaboration with the Colombian government, had prepared well, avoiding trouble in spite of unfriendly jeers from some of the crowds. There were also demonstrations in front of our hotel.

"After Bogotá, we flew to Caracas. When we got off the airplane there, we saw a good-sized crowd waiting for us. There was some question as to whether we'd get off at the end of the airport or go directly to the airport terminal and deplane there, which is what we finally did."

The trip had been problematic from the beginning, but Rubottom says that Caracas was where the real fireworks began. "The date was May 14, 1958. We arrived mid-morning after a short flight, landing at the main airport on the coast, and it was a 30-minute drive up a steep incline to the capital city. Demonstrators surrounded the airplane on landing, and the Vice-Presidential party had to be escorted to a secure building under heavy guard. We passed under a balcony where the Vice-President and Mrs. Nixon were spat upon from above, as were those accompanying them.

"We got into big Cadillac sedans, the Vice-President and Chief of Protocol in one, and Mrs. Nixon in the second one. The Ambassador and I rode in the third. At the top of the incline, our procession slowed down to enter the city limits. At that point, the cars were surrounded by dozens if not hundreds of demonstrators, who began rocking the cars, trying to overturn them. The members of the U.S. Secret Service who were with us showed great courage in the way they handled matters. People were beating on the windows with sticks, and there were some whom the Secret Service couldn't fend off. Fortunately, there were enough Venezuelan security police to push away the mob so that the Embassy car could keep moving, even though quite slowly.

During his 1958 tour of South America, Nixon and his entourage—including Rubottom—faced street protests. This photograph was taken in Caracas.

By inter-car radio communication, the Vice-President was asked to change his itinerary, going directly to the American residence atop a hill in the city, and omitting the scheduled visit to lay a wreath at Bolivar's tomb. Shaken, he agreed.

"I must say that Vice-President and Mrs. Nixon conducted themselves with great dignity and courage in those circumstances. But we were all quite stunned by this hostility and by this obscene gesture of spitting on the U.S. Vice-President."

Rubottom recalls that it wasn't until after the group had passed the angry mob that he had a chance to collect his thoughts. "I realized that there was no telling what would have happened had the demonstrators succeeded in breaking into the car and getting at the Vice-President," he says. "There was a great concentration of people, and the streets were very narrow. So we voided our original planned route and went directly to the embassy residence, where we stayed from then on.

"However, somewhere between 10:00 in the morning, shortly after we arrived, and perhaps 2:00 in the afternoon—or about the time we were finishing lunch—there was a four-hour hiatus within which, for perhaps an hour, we weren't talking to Washington. Washington was very concerned for that hour. They had read these earlier reports, all the wire reports, and the Vice-President's security and safety were a very real concern.

"I talked to Washington on the phone half a dozen times while we were there. There was a question of whether the demonstrators would try to come up the hill to where the embassy residence was. We really didn't know for a while whether the Vice-President was going to be secure. I went off and conferred and came back, and I was told the next time I telephoned Washington that President Eisenhower had ordered the Marines to be on alert, and he'd actually had them flown from some place in North Carolina to San

Juan and to Guantanamo, to be ready for take-off in the event such was necessary.

"This came as a shock to us, and it cast another cloud over our already troubled visit. Whatever feeling of contrition and concern the Venezuelans had had about the threat on the life of the U.S. Vice-President vanished and was replaced by their immediate concern, as Latin Americans, that we were threatening to send the Marines in. To the Venezuelans, the very mention of Marines raised the threat of military intervention."

Yet Rubottom understands why Washington took this step, and he believes history will bear out that it was not an unwise move. "But I also understand the adverse public reaction that it caused throughout Latin America," he says. "Frankly, I don't know how decision-makers can ever find a balance between those two viewpoints. The decision to send in the Marines was made at the presidential level, of course with State Department cooperation.

"I think there was some reluctance, at the highest level of the State Department, about taking military action. I have a feeling, though, that Under-Secretary Robert Murphy and the Joint Chiefs and the Department of Defense and probably the CIA, all of whom I think were involved in the recommending process, probably favored this. If I'd been there, I'm not at all sure but what I would have favored it myself. It would be presumptuous to say I wouldn't have, under those conditions. But we did not recommend it from the field, and we didn't know about it until it was already done. The final decision was announced by the President, and the Vice-President was quite dismayed when he heard about it. He kept this to himself, of course, but he was upset, and the rest of us were, too. And in any case, by the time this back-up had been ordered and deployed, we realized we didn't need it any more."

The delegation left South America soon after, more or

less on schedule. They flew back to the United States, and, Dick says, "We were relieved to make it home."

The next several months brought numerous conferences and high-level conversations about the trip and the events the delegation had experienced. Rubottom says, "There were countless discussions by the Senate Foreign Relations Committee, as well as mountains of papers and books written about those events."

The United States was blindsided by the hostility Vice-President Nixon and the others in the group confronted in South America, because they had been completely unaware

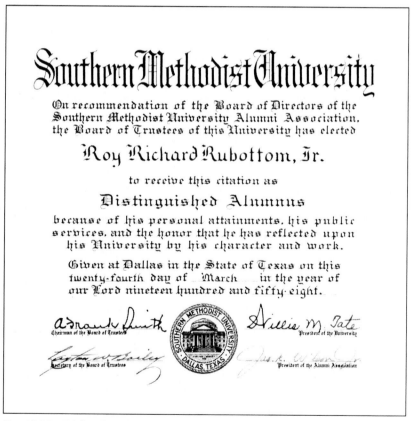

In 1958, Richard Rubottom was named a Distinguished Alumnus of S.M.U.

of these negative attitudes. With the realizations this trip brought, the Eisenhower administration was forced into a period of self-examination.

Says Rubottom, "I don't think we ever quite got to the point of acknowledging publicly that everything we'd done prior to that time was wrong or misguided. We didn't say that we would immediately change all our policies toward South America, based on the lessons we had learned on this trip. But it did happen that our policies were different after that. Vice-President Nixon's trip to South America opened people's eyes to how serious the alienation between the U.S. and many parts of Latin America actually was. Diplomats and lawmakers reflected on whether the negative attitudes had come about as a result of some policy we'd followed or not followed in the region."

Regardless of what prompted it, Rubottom thought the re-examination of U.S. attitudes toward Latin America was a good thing. He says, "As assistant Secretary, I had been turned down for two straight years in my efforts to get fairly modest increases in our budget for the U.S. Information Service, as carried out in the field. Why? Because I had been fighting this low priority rating. Suddenly we were high priority, which meant that we were able to get more money, which in turn allowed us to reflect on other aspects of our policy—aspects beyond budget and information gathering.

"Funding for the Voice of America and the information program were vastly increased, as those concerns moved from the lowest priority to the highest, which only under-lines the significance of that trip in influencing U.S. policies towards Latin America."

Rubottom says that among the lessons the United States learned was this: Throughout a major diplomatic trip like the Vice-President's, behind-the-scenes decisions are con-stantly being made, by diplomats and state department officials and security officials who are always assessing the leader's safety. Since universities were popular gathering places for demonstrators, decisions about which universities Vice-President Nixon would visit had become a complicated question during the trip. In Peru, for example, the entourage was informed that there might be violence if they went to San Marcos. The recommendation was made that they not go there.

Yet Rubottom describes that recommendation as vague, recalling, "It could not be backed up with anything definite. If we didn't go, I thought it would look as though we were bending over backwards to avoid confrontations. Also, the public itinerary had already been announced, and it indicated that we were going there. If we hadn't, it would have been obvious that we were running out, fearful of the consequences of meeting these demonstrators. So we had to make the very delicate judgment as to whether we'd rather take a risk, or show fear in the face of what might or might not be a threat. Ultimately, we decided he should go, and I think that was the right decision."

When the delegation returned to the United States, and, for that matter, even while they were still in South America, considerable media attention was given to the dramatic events of Vice-President Nixon's visit. As is often the case, opinion makers tried to find someone to blame, and a few settled on Richard Rubottom.

Rubottom reflected on these matters in a letter to his mother on June 8, 1958:

We have never doubted for a moment that all our loved ones in the family were thinking about us and sharing the interest the rest of the country has in 'our' problems involving Latin America. We have realized that there might be one or two of the stories in the newspapers that would attract your concern. . . Obviously, my position as Assistant Secretary is at the sufferance of the President and the Secretary of State. However, the Vice-President paid me a very nice compliment in his speech before the National Press Club two weeks ago and has never shown any indication of irritation or discontent with my role during his Latin-American trip. Both the President and the Secretary have gone out of their way to say nice things to me recently and I have every reason to believe I can stay on working in my present assignment for a while longer, if that is my wish.

The nature of the work Rubottom did for the State Department, as liaison between the United States and a volatile region of the world, meant that he was always in somebody's line of fire. Yet he moved through the vicissitudes of this scrutiny with grace, owing to his deep understanding of right and wrong. He concluded the above letter to his mother by writing,

The fundamental thing, of course, is not the nice things said, but the way I feel deep inside my mind and conscience. In that respect, I have been quite calm and unruffled about the developments. We have had serious economic problems in Latin America for the past year and a half or two years. Many things that we might have done before now to alleviate the problems there, we simply have not been able to get the decisions made in the Government and in the Congress to move toward those solutions. We are making fast progress now, however, and this is one of the positive accomplishments of the unfortunate treatment accorded the Nixons on their South American tour.

It always bothered Rubottom that the United States was accused of supporting dictators, and that accusation was again leveled on this South American trip. He also addressed this issue in the letter to his mother:

> *We have not in the last several years done anything to 'support' dictators. We have many interests that require that we get along, at least properly and correctly, with the governments of this hemisphere, irrespective of the form of government they maintain, which, after all, is the responsibility of the people of those countries themselves. My whole background and personal philosophy is slanted toward the same democratic free principles that we follow here in the United States. I believe that we must improve our example, and that we should maintain relations with all governments as one of the best means of influencing them constructively toward more democratic freedoms; but obviously they are not all going to have exactly the same kind of democracy we do.*

For years after his harrowing trip to South America with the Vice-President, Rubottom pondered the character of Nixon the man. "Richard Nixon was the complete political animal," he says, "always attuned to the most delicate nuances of any situation, always looking for political advantage. He was distant and, as was revealed in the Watergate tapes, ready to sacrifice those closest to him if need be. In that respect, he stood in sharp contrast to some of the other political leaders I was privileged to know, leaders such as President Eisenhower and Secretaries of State Marshall, Dulles, Herter, and Rusk."

One by-product of Rubottom's trip to South America was that his position began to receive a lot more attention. The *Houston Post*, for example, began a long profile of Rubottom in the Sunday edition, on October 5, 1958, this way:

Barely over 10 years ago, Roy Richard Rubottom, Jr., was on the threshold of a quiet new career as a promising young officer in a state bank in Corsicana.

Today, Rubottom rules, from a thick-carpeted office in the State Department, an administrative force of 1,000 people who carry American policies into the lives of millions of South and Central Americans, from the Rio Grande to the Straits of Magellan.

Rubottom's position as Assistant Secretary of State for Inter-American Affairs is one of the hot seats in Washington. Weaving through the tangled affairs of our Latin-American neighbors has never been an easy task. But the rioting of last spring in the midst of Vice-President Richard M. Nixon's tour has brought the office squarely before the nation.

Air travel provided an efficient way for Dick and Billy Ruth to get to the meetings they were required to attend.

Years later, on August 9, 1974, the day Nixon resigned the U.S. presidency, Rubottom again found himself thinking about the life and career of Richard Nixon. In the following journal entry, Rubottom recalls his personal experience with the President, and ponders Nixon's history-making resignation. He detailed his 1958 trip with Nixon from the longer view, for time had passed, and his studied response demonstrates how time shapes thinking about history.

I am writing this on the day Richard M. Nixon is expected to announce either his resignation or his decision to vacate the office of the Presidency in order that Vice-President Ford might take over the Presidential functions under terms of the 25th Amendment to the Constitution. Should Nixon fail to take one or the other of those actions, he is certain to be impeached and convicted by the Congress of the United States of America.

How do I feel on this historic day? Like most Americans, certainly, I feel shocked, numbed, and incredulous, even though I've had two years to prepare for this possibility. In fact, until the House Judiciary Committee hearings began last month, followed by a unanimous Supreme Court decision requiring the President to turn over all requested taped conversations to the Special Prosecutor, I seriously questioned whether the President would even be impeached, let alone convicted. It was his own admission of having lied to the American people about his two-year cover-up effort that brought the shocking realization—and this only three days ago—that Nixon was finished as President.

Few Americans, even those who hate Nixon, and I have known several whose feelings went to that limit, will not pause, at least for a moment, before the tragedy that has befallen the man, and the nation. The nation will survive, and its resiliency may surprise us all. The *man, however, has suffered a crushing blow, and one could wish it were possible to convey some sense of vicarious suffering, more than sympathy, to him and his family. It has never happened before, at least in this country, that a man has fallen so far—and all in public view. There have been other political trials, but the one I remember most vividly, that of the ex-Mayor of New York, William O'Dwyer,* was over in a day. The trials of Nixon—both the indirect one, through the media, and, more recently, the [literal one before the] House Committee—and also the indirect trial affecting his principal subordinates—all these have been unceasing, hour after hour, day after day, for well over a year.*

For me, at least, the United States Presidency has always transcended the mere mortal who happened to be President at any given time. I saw Franklin D. Roosevelt once as a college youth, and later I was enraptured by his pre-W.W.II "fireside chats." I served in the Navy while he was its Commander-in-Chief. I joined the Foreign Service under the Presidency of Harry Truman, and saw him at close hand a few times. It was my privilege to work closely on many occasions with President Eisenhower, and later to know and serve under Presidents Kennedy and Johnson. I have not had direct contact with Nixon while he has been President, although our paths crossed briefly in Dallas during his 1968 campaign.

In some ways, however, I have known Nixon better than the rest because I endured pain and unfair treatment at his hands. Even so, I have respected the Presidency while he has occupied it, and I regret his fall.

---

*William O'Dwyer was mayor of New York in the late 1940s. His administration was tarnished by accusations of his connection to a police corruption scandal. He resigned his office and was later appointed U.S. Ambassador to Mexico, but the corruption charges dogged him for the remainder of his political career.

My recollections of my experiences with Nixon are quite vivid. They occurred while he was Vice-President under Dwight Eisenhower. I was Assistant Secretary of State for Inter-American Affairs, and I accompanied him on his 1958 tour of South America. My understanding of Nixon is based principally on my observations of him during those eight arduous days.

Later, in his book, Six Crises, *Nixon reported deprecatingly of my performance in that position, and [he] actually told one untruth in recalling our joint experience in Lima, Peru.*

Nixon had few confidants, relying almost completely on his immediate staff for advice and assistance. This became clear, and crucial, when we started to plan the details for that trip, which was to include eight countries. Our country desk officers at the State Department prepared detailed briefing material on each country to be visited, but we had virtually no direct access to the Vice-President before departure. Thus he got his briefing indirectly, through his staff, who were not knowledgeable about South America.

Once [the trip was] underway, Nixon would listen to the Ambassador's advice in a given capital city, then consult his staff privately before making his decisions about schedules, calls, security measures, and other important details. In some instances, he did not follow the advice of the Ambassador, let alone mine. In one such case, at our first stop in Montevideo, the result was almost certainly harmful to the last three stops of his trip.

Nixon enjoyed the pomp and ceremony that accompanied him everywhere he went in public. He ably discharged the ceremonial duties of his office, and usually he could be depended on to say and do what was demanded by the occasion. Occasionally, though, he erred by overstating. The plush treatment, including gourmet meals, accorded him by the U.S. military and diplomatic establishment was clearly expected and desired by Nixon. Yet Vice-President and Mrs. Nixon were very considerate of me during our time together on the 10-passenger military aircraft. They usually invited me to eat with them at their special table. Our discussions ranged the field, from international affairs to the relative advantages of public and private school education for children. Their behavior was exemplary.

Nixon was vitally concerned about his press relations. He gave that subject high priority and showed his displeasure if anything went wrong. He resorted to such actions as kicking a soccer ball at the start of a game in Quito in order to get public attention, and there he succeeded.

Nixon showed great courage and calm, as did Mrs. Nixon, during the tension-filled hours in Caracas, especially during the attempt to stop and overturn his car at the entrance to the city. Later, in discussions at the Embassy Residence with Ambassador Sparks and me, when it was touch-and-go as to whether to leave, or to remain for part of the schedule in Caracas, the Vice-President made the best of what had to be for him a galling situation.

But I maintain that the Caracas incident could have been avoided. I knew it then, and I know it now, and I believe that incident reveals quite a lot about Richard Nixon.

Dick and Billy Ruth attended many formal dances in Washington, D.C.

CHAPTER 11

Becoming an Ambassador

When Vice-President Nixon returned from his trip to Latin America, he reported that the threat of Communism in Latin America had increased. Asked today whether he agreed with Nixon's assessment in 1958, Rubottom says, "Yes. Communism had been present in Latin America for a long time. The center of Communism in Latin America had moved from capital to capital. At one time, during World War II and right after, it was in Mexico. Even earlier, perhaps, Havana was the capital of the Latin-American Communists. Most people don't realize that Batista, for example, had Communists in his Cabinet, and even Machado did, in 1934, before he was overthrown. So Communist work had long been done in Cuba and throughout Latin America."

Rubottom goes on to note that by 1958, Montevideo, one of the places where the Russians had an embassy, had become another center of organized Communism. He explains, "I'm speaking here about aggressive international Communism, working through the Soviets. Anybody who questions [whether this was going on], I think, is naïve. I realize there's also a grassroots type of Communism, and there are certain branches of ultra-Marxist types and so-called Black Communists and, even by the late 1950s, I

169

suppose—since they really hadn't had the break with the Communist Chinese—there were also some Maoist-type, Peking-type Communists beginning to splinter off. The Communist threat was becoming more visible throughout the world in the late 1950s and throughout the 1960s."

It was against this backdrop that President Dwight D. Eisenhower appointed Richard Rubottom U.S. Ambassador to Argentina in 1960. Eleanor and Rick were in private schools, so they became boarders while their parents and eight-year-old John moved to Buenos Aires and Dick began his new responsibilities. Both Dick and Billy Ruth wrote long, detailed letters to Eleanor and Rick (see Chapter 13), in which they gave their impressions of Argentina and the life there.

Rubottom greets Adolfo López Mateos, who was president of Mexico from 1958-64.

Reading these letters, as well as Dick's speeches from this period, it is easy to ascertain the Rubottoms' excitement about their new position, as well as their enduring warmth toward the people of Latin America.

From the moment he arrived in Argentina, Dick began reaching out to people. His command of Spanish gave him an advantage as he went to town meetings, traveled to small villages in remote regions of the country, and extended the hand of U.S. friendship to officials high and low.

As they always had, the Rubottoms became involved in a local church, where they taught Sunday School. John was enrolled in The American School, where he began making friends as the family settled into their new life.

Asked how he viewed his promotion to U.S. Ambass-

Rubottom and Guillermo Sevilla-Sacasa, Dean of the Diplomatic Corps. This photo was taken just before the Rubottoms moved to Argentina for Dick to assume the ambassadorship.

ador, Dick says, "I knew that being an ambassador represented the top level of assignment. I knew it was a very demanding job, and that I'd have to be on my toes all the time. You're the representative of the President of the United States when you're an ambassador, looked up to and respected by virtue of that assignment, whether or not you do it well."

Unfortunately, however, internecine squabbling and instability were endemic in Argentine politics during Rubottom's years as Ambassador. Arturo Frondizi, whose inauguration Rubottom had attended during that 1958 South American tour with Vice-President Richard Nixon, was the democratically elected president. However, the ideas of Juan Perón still held sway with many Argentines,

Upon arrival in Buenos Aires in 1960, Dick, Billy Ruth, and John Rubottom visited the United States Information Service.

and a number of Peronists continued to function in official roles. The Argentine military, meanwhile, was staunchly opposed to Peronism and Peronists. This dynamic led to warring factions within government, with one side, led by Alvaro Alsogaray, representing the military, and the other, headed by Rogelio Frigerio, functioning as a voice for the

1960. Billy Ruth meeting Arturo Frondizi, President of Argentina.

The Rubottoms hosted esteemed South American writer Jorge Luis Borges and his wife. Buenos Aires, 1960.

Rubottom is at far left; President Frondizi of Argentina seated in the center; and Edward Kennedy, on a visit to Argentina representing his brother, second from the right.

When Dick was Ambassador to Argentina, the whole family assembled for a portrait.

Entertaining at the Embassy Residence, 1960.

The Rubottoms made extensive efforts to reach out to local officials as well as to Argentineans at all levels of society. Here, they host local leaders at the Embassy Residence. 1961.

Billy Ruth Rubottom often entertained diplomats' wives.

Peronist forces. Frondizi had to find a way to incorporate, or at least mollify, these factions.

During the summer of 1961, Bayless Manning, a professor at Yale Law School, visited Argentina. His responsibilities at Yale included Latin-American developments, notably in the legal field, and in that capacity he was invited by the Argentine Undersecretary of Interior, Dr. Guillermo Acuna Anzorena, to visit Argentina and get to know her people. In a memo written on his return, Professor Manning wrote about what he had observed in Argentina.

"Rogelio Frigerio is still very influential in the government and apparently indispensable to Frondizi," he wrote. Pointing to the warring factions vying for power, Professor Manning went on to observe, "The Argentine political scene is Byzantine and convoluted in the atmosphere of mistrust and maneuver that permeates it. This might not be apparent to an American who had only limited or periodic contact with Argentine political figures."

The professor's contact, however, was neither limited nor periodic. In fact, he was plunged into an intensity of exposure to individuals in power, and his memo makes clear that the views and observations of the people he spoke with left him with the impression that "duplicity is an ingrained part of the Argentine political character and its functioning."

Within months of his arrival, Rubottom, too, found himself pulled into the vortex of Argentine politics. Because he was well-connected with people in widely varied segments of Argentine society, he saw conflicts in an even-handed, analytical way. At one point, as the representative of the U.S. government, Rubottom tried to apprise President Frondizi and his cadre of the strength of their enemies, but bad news just led Frondizi to blame the messenger. This article from *Time Magazine* elucidates the tangled sequence of events:

Out Goes Rubottom

Time Magazine
October 20, 1961

The old names and old faces that dominated U.S. Policy in Latin America before the Alliance for Progress are fading fast. Last week the time came for Roy Richard Rubottom, Jr., 49, Assistant Secretary of State for Inter-American Affairs from 1957 to 1960, who was dropped as Ambassador to Argentina. As a holdover diplomat from the previous administration, Rubottom submitted a pro forma resignation last January. Last week President Kennedy accepted it.

All Bases

A top White House aide described Rubottom's removal as nothing more than the natural replacement of Eisenhower appointees with New Frontiersmen. There was more to it. Taking advantage of his excellent command of Spanish from the moment he reached Argentina, Rubottom rushed forth to tell the U.S. story to every Argentine he could buttonhole. He held round-table talks at the embassy residence with labor leaders, students, civic groups. He talked with governors, legislators, deputies, mayors, politicians and plain citizens. He delivered lectures, taught Sunday school, traveled to more remote reaches of Argentina than any previous U.S. diplomat, and met record numbers of Argentines from every level of society.

But in his zealous efforts to touch every base, Rubottom, apparently unconsciously, got involved in a palace faction fight.

At the head of one faction stood Rogelio Frigerio, the political grey eminence who kept in touch with the Peronists for President Arturo Frondizi and dreamed up such international attention getters as Argentina's offer of "good offices" as a mediator to settle the differences between Castro's Cuba and the U.S.

Leading the other group was Alvaro Alsogaray, the conservative, army-supported economic planner forced upon Frondizi by the anti-Perón military brass.

Clear Hints

Rubottom had, not unnaturally, favored the Alsogaray faction. When the Frigerio group launched an attack on Planner Alsogaray, Rubottom warned high Argentine officials that the economist's dismissal might scare off the U.S. private investment. When Frigerio got his bright idea of mediating the Castro-Kennedy quarrel, Frigerio blamed Rubottom for the polite U.S. dismissal of the offer. During Adlai Stevenson's visit to Argentina last June, Frondizi hinted that an ambassadorial change might be a good idea. Frondizi got the same message across in his talks with Kennedy three weeks ago.

Last week, on one of his forays outside Buenos Aires, Rubottom plunked a 100 peso chip on No. 35 at the Mar del Plata casino, and watched almost wistfully as the roulette ball dropped neatly into the 35 slot. At least, he said, collecting 3,500 pesos, "nobody can deny that my assignment in Argentina didn't end with a lucky stroke."

Next post: State Department adviser at the Naval War College at Newport, R.I.

After Frondizi made clear to President Kennedy that he'd like to see a new U.S. Ambassador to Argentina, a flurry of telegrams passed between Rubottom and Washington. Dick was held in high regard at the State Department, and it was evident to everyone that he was being treated unfairly. Secretary of State Dean Rusk and officials throughout the Department understood that Argentine politics had simply overtaken Rubottom, and that his possible transfer from that post was no reflection on his competence or his integrity.

In that exchange of telegrams during the months leading up to Dick's resignation, his perspective on events is made clear in official-sounding, truncated diplomacy-speak. Even so, the telegrams leave little doubt about the precariousness of the government then in power in Argentina.

Adding to these destabilizing events was the fact that Frondizi was meeting with Che Guevara, and the U.S. government feared an alliance there. At the same time, the United States was in a dangerous stand-off with Cuba, and Frondizi's advisor, Frigerio, who was clearly allied with Cuba, pressed to mediate between the Cuba and the U.S. This meant the precarious U.S.–Cuba conundrum was pulled in to events unfolding in Argentina. Behind every meeting, every letter, telegram, or sit-down during those hot summer months of 1961 were layer upon layer of delicate diplomacy, hidden agendas, and vested interests from around the globe.

Following are excerpts from only a few of countless telegrams and memoranda of conversation in which Rubottom names names and gives dates as he describes the historic events swirling around him.

As the messages make clear, things were happening fast. But even in the storm of events, the tone and syntax of the telegrams suggest what all parties understood: in diplomatic work, these things happen, and *when* they happen they have little to do with individuals and everything to do with governments and the balance of power. Ambassadors could be frank in official telegrams, which in any case were classified, but their public face was always to support whatever decision Washington made.

August 22, 1961
Telegram from Rubottom to Washington

President Frondizi's latest crisis, which is the result of his own doing, is another example of Machiavellian tactics at which he is considered expert, but which continue to embroil him in domestic difficulties as well as international embarrassment. USG [United States Government] can try to understand, at times even sympathize, especially when Argentine military takes exaggerated, golpista position, but Frondizi tactics exceed friendly bounds when he tries irresponsibly to blame U.S. for his troubles. This he clearly did in talking to Argentine military leaders last Sunday and in obviously calculated leaks to press. . .

Frondizi continues to operate with regular Government and with shadow government headed by Frigerio. . . .

President Frondizi would like USG to applaud every move he makes. His speech last night, recalling President Kennedy's statement when Minister Alemann visited him on May 24, again reveals importance he places on U.S. approval his policies. . . . There are times, however, when we cannot and should not adopt a completely uncritical attitude.

. . .Irresponsible charges against me could be ignored were it not for other factors. Hope this will be helpful to you in analyzing complex Argentine situation.

August 30, 1961
From American Cable & Radio System

THE CHAMBER OF COMMERCE OF THE UNITED STATES IN THE ARGENTINE REPUBLIC IS DEEPLY CONCERNED OVER PRESS REPORTS INDICATING THE PROBABLE REPLACEMENT OF AMBASSADOR RUBOTTOM STOP THE MEMBERS OF OUR CHAMBER HAVE HAD FREQUENT OPPORTUNITY TO ASSESS HIS OUTSTANDING QUALIFICATIONS IN REPRESENTING OUR COUNTRY BEFORE THE ARGENTINE GOVERNMENT AND THE ARGENTINE PUBLIC AS WELL AS WITH COMMERCIAL LABOR EDUCATIONAL AND OTHER CIRCLES STOP HIS DEMONSTRATED PROFESSIONAL SKILL AND LONG EXPERIENCE HAVE THE ENTHUSIASTIC AND WHOLEHEARTED SUP-

PORT OF THE AMERICAN COMMUNITY AND BUSINESS IN-
TERESTS HERE STOP HIS DEEP KNOWLEDGE OF LATIN
AMERICAN PSHYCHOLOGY AND OF THE SPANISH LAN-
GUAGE HAVE EARNED HIM THE FULL RESPECT OF THE AR-
GENTINE PUBLIC STOP WE SUBMIT THAT FREQUENT
CHANGES OF AMBASSADORS ARE HIGHLY DISTURBING
AND WE HOLD THAT ANOTHER CHANGE AT THIS TIME
WOULD BE GREATLY DETRIMENTAL TO DEVELOPING PRO-
GRAMS AND PUBLIC RELATIONS STOP WE RESPECTFULLY
SUGGEST THAT THE BEST INTERESTS OF THE UNITED
STATES WILL BE SERVED BY AMBASSADOR RUBOTTOM'S
CONTINUANCE IN ARGENTINA AND THE AMERICAN CHAM-
BER OF COMMERCE RESPECTFULLY SO RECOMMENDS.

BOARD OF GOVERNORS

USCHAMBCOM

September 1, 1961
Telegram from Rubottom to Washington

Following spontaneous message from several organiza-
tions endorsing me. Press and others beginning focus on domestic Argentine maneuverings believed back of my possible transfer. This subject lead editorial today's *La Prensa*.
Rumors more public comments in similar vein imminent.
Thus my replacement has now become question transcend-
ing administrative personnel change, and has taken on
larger dimension affecting total U.S. interest in Argentina,
including effectiveness of whomever may be Ambassador.

As Embassy has reported regularly, there is widespread
domestic criticism of GOA [Government of Argentina] foreign policy, both its substance and its administration, publicly identifies with FRIGERIO forces. This criticism has
been intensifying as result U.S. exposé [of] falsity [of]
Frigerio group rationale behind Frondizi-Guevara meeting.

Frigerio forces, long identified with neutralist moves and effort deflect U.S. from current Cuban policy, have made little effort [to] disguise their attempts [to] cause my recall since last March. Following Punta del Este Conference, various newspapermen informed Embassy officers that Argentine delegation openly spoke of my imminent transfer and implied they had arranged it.

. . . Eduardo Garcia, President Argentine Chamber of Commerce, just told Embassy Counselor that Chamber's Press Representative urged by representatives of *Clarin* and *Noticias Graficas* to withhold yesterday's release supporting me. Neither paper published it. Their representatives told Chamber's press man that endorsement of me would implicate Chamber in a plot allegedly inspired by me for military overthrow of Government. Garcia told Counselor that no serious person would believe this but such stories circulated among journalists of these two pro-Government newspapers reflect Frigerio Machiavellian tactics.

Senior staff members and I have been told by *Alsogaray, del Pablo Pardo, La Prensa's editor, Correo de la Tarde's Manrique*, and *Eduardo Garcia* that it is an open secret among informed Argentine sources that Frigerio and associates have been irritated by my failure to play their game and support or remain silent in face of their fabrications with respect U.S. Policy. They have said Frigerio enraged at my failure when questioned by Cabinet officials and need-to-know persons to do other than to deny that U.S. was consulted in advance with respect March offer good offices [*referring to Frigerio's offer to mediate between the U.S. and Cuba—an offer the U.S., through Rubottom, politely declined*] or that U.S. endorsed it. Same sources, through their own intelligence, aware of falsity of rationale offered by MUGICA, as gullible mouthpiece for Frigerio group, for Frondizi-Guevara meeting to effect this was "encouraged" by U.S. and preceded by secret Goodwin-Guevara meeting in Uruguay.

These and other proven U.S. friends have expressed concern at prospect that not only can Frigerio control the nomination of Argentine Ambassadors, but also influence the designation or tenure of service of the U.S. Ambassador to Argentina.

September 26, 1961
Confidential Memorandum [of Conversation between Presidents Kennedy and Frondizi]

President Frondizi said that Argentine public opinion was evolving towards a better understanding of American policy, and that with a joint, friendly, and common effort, success could be achieved, but that it was necessary to be able to count on political support in Argentina. Therefore, it was important that the representatives of the United States in Argentina be able to interpret President Kennedy's ideas and philosophy and that they not cause problems for the Argentine government.

President Kennedy said that at the present time, the selection of a new Ambassador to Argentina was being considered, and that the new Ambassador would be selected with great care.

President Frondizi said that naturally the American Government would be the one to decide on who was going to be Ambassador, but that he wanted to speak frankly about this matter. He said that the United States needed a representative in Argentina who had a feeling for President Kennedy's Latin-American policy, especially with reference to Argentina. He said that the success or failure of American policy in Latin America would affect everybody.

President Frondizi said that he wanted to return to Argentina now on the basis of an agreement on basic issues, in order to be able to inform the Argentine people that his conversations with President Kennedy showed that the United States supported Argentina's economic and social problems. He said that the success or failure of Argentina's experience, with American support, would be an example for the other Latin-American countries.

. . . President Frondizi said that he thought that it was important that there be personal contacts between President Kennedy and him about the problems affecting Latin America.

[The above is an excerpt from Page 4 of the original Memorandum of Conversation.]

September 30, 1961
Telegram, Washington to Rubottom
Eyes only for Ambassador Rubottom
Limited distribution

White House plans announce first week October the president accepts your resignation as ambassador Argentina. At same time department plans make press statement regarding your assignment as faculty adviser Naval War College. Text both announcements will be sent to you in advance so that if desirable you may make appropriate statement locally when announcements made here.

Secretary most appreciative your willingness serve as faculty adviser Naval War College. As Roger Jones informed you, Secretary attaches great importance to filling position as faculty adviser at the four armed services colleges with top flight officers who have served as ambassadors. Chief Naval Operations insistent that department immediately make available faculty adviser for Naval War College. While we recognize early move to Newport will cause personal inconvenience to you and create some official problems, request you make plans complete official leave-taking and consultation department to enable you if at all possible take up new duties by October 23.

October 3, 1961
Rubottom to Washington

Plan depart BA all reasonable speed once announcement made, but can do nothing until then. You fully aware essential amenities required dignified leave-taking. . . . Would like sail SS *Brazil* Oct 23 arriving NY Nov 7. Advise if satisfactory.

Next day, October 4, 1961
Secretary of State Dean Rusk to Rubottom [previous correspondence was with Assistant Secretary Bowles]

Deeply regret unable meet your wishes regarding later arrival in U.S. Naval War College term underway several weeks and chief Naval Operations extremely disturbed at delay has personally appealed White House help in having dept make officer available Newport immediately.

White House announcement will be made next day or so and state in substance that your resignation being accepted and that you are being given another assignment. Will cable or telephone immediately time fixed. Dept will not issue press release but answer press queries along following lines:

Ambassador Rubottom's resignation has been under consideration by president for several months as have resignations of other ambassadors appointed by previous administration. As announced by White House president has now decided accept Mr. Rubottom's resignation.

Secretary is pleased Amb Rubottom has agreed serve as state dept adviser at Naval War College at Newport, Rhode

Island. This is one of four senior officer training schools of armed services and dept, at request of armed services, assigns officers to serve as senior faculty advisors on international affairs at each school. It is Secretary's strong desire fill these positions with high-ranking officers of good background and experience.

If asked whether a decision has yet been made with respect to new amb for Argentina, dept will reply that an announcement will be made in due course.

Suggest you leave Buenos Aires by plane October 21 or 21, spend Oct 23 here on consultation, and report Newport Oct 24. This give you only slightly less time for orderly leave-taking than you proposed, but would unfortunately preclude your having well-deserved rest which return by boat would provide. You will be order back to Wash for further consultation if dept or you desire. There will be recess of War College from December 16 to New Years.

Realize these plans involve real sacrifice on your part and most grateful for your attitude.

October 5, 1961
Rubottom to Washington

. . .When Washington announcement made, I plan to issue following statement:

My family and I have had the extremely good fortune to have lived in Argentina for the past year. To hold the post of Ambassador here, and to reside in your deservedly famed capital city of Buenos Aires, has been an honor and a privilege. The interest which we have in Argentina—a brave, vigorous nation of people at once *simpatico* and possessed of profound spiritual qualities—has deepened into genuine affection. We are grateful for the generous hospitality and friendship that have been extended to us everywhere, in your capital city as well as the many provinces we have visited.

Living in Argentina, traveling through the country, and talking with the people, one cannot help but be struck by how few and how minor are the differences between our two peoples, and how many and how great are the similarities. I find it, therefore, most encouraging and most gratifying to be able to observe that the relations between Argentina and the United States are not only at the highest level ever, but [also they] show every sign of remaining that way.

My next assignment will afford me the opportunity to combine my experience as a Naval officer, in which capacity I started my career in government, with that of the diplomatic service.

I hope to return to Argentina sometime in the future.

And just that quickly, Billy Ruth and Dick found themselves preparing for another move, this time to New England. They looked forward to being close to their children (Eleanor was a student at Pembroke, and Rick was at Phillips Exeter), re-connecting with old friends, and being on the same continent, at least, as most of their family.

Before they left, though, Dick gave a farewell speech, in which he exhibited the grace and discretion that had marked his entire diplomatic career:

> *Thank you all very much for your kind words about my wife and me.*
>
> *Today I leave Argentina as much with a feeling of satisfaction as of sorrow. Satisfaction because of the excellent and uninterrupted relations and the development of mutual understanding between our two countries; and sorrow for having to bid farewell to the many friends that my wife and I have here. But my stay over the last year has not been my first and will not be my last. I had*

visited Argentina before and I trust that I will visit again, more than once, in the future. So more than saying "goodbye," I would like to say "until we meet again."

This is the Rubottoms' farewell party for all Embassy staff in Buenos Aires.

Professionally, during this year which I have served my country as Ambassador to the Republic of Argentina, my rewards have been many. I have the highest consideration for the functionaries of the Argentine government with whom I have worked. I have visited many of Argentina's provinces and I have conversed with Argentines of every social class; and as much in this beautiful capitol as in the provinces, I have been able personally to see innumerable tests of the firm determination of the Argentine people to turn the formidable potential of this nation into a palpable reality. I hope that, for my part, I will be able to make known, in some way, the character of my own compatriots and of the traditions and aspirations of my country.

Time can be sensed in many ways. One minute can seem like eternity, one day can have the fleetingness of an instant. In a certain way, this year has seemed very brief. But in another way, the professional satisfactions and the uncountable manifestations of personal friendship that I have had the good fortune of enjoying represent much more than many enjoy over the course of a lifetime. So to the many of you who are here and others who are absent, my family and I send our profound and sincere thanks.

Only a few months after the Rubottoms moved to Rhode Island, events in Argentina reached the boiling point, when Peronists, increasingly fearful of a Communist coup, aligned with the military. The dénouement came during the Cuban Missile Crisis, when Communist elements and radical leftists became vociferous in their demands for support of Cuba. Frondizi remained neutral in the matter.

Then, on March 28, 1962, while he was attending a Pan American summit, Frondizi was deposed from office by a coup d'état.

Dick Rubottom, whom Frondizi had declared *persona non grata* before he left Argentina, was not surprised at this news.

This was taken inside the embassy residence.

CHAPTER 12

Naval War College
1961–1964

Settled in a cozy two-story wooden house with a big yard and a draft in winter, the Rubottoms soon felt at home in Newport. The State Department delivered their furniture and effects, and they fixed up an attic room for Rick, and rooms on the second floor for John and Eleanor. Billy Ruth started a garden, planting vegetables and flowers. Dick, Billy, and John all looked forward to the weekends and holidays that Eleanor and Rick came to visit from school.

Although they had never had the opportunity to sail before, Dick and Billy Ruth started learning how on the sailboats available at the War College. They found they loved it, and soon all three of the children also became sailing enthusiasts. During their time at the Naval War College, the Rubottoms spent many happy hours on the water, both as a family and with friends. During the warmer months, in fact, Billy Ruth would meet Dick during their lunch hour and they would picnic on Narragansett Bay.

Meanwhile, Dick felt grateful for the chance to be at the Naval War College and think deeply about all that had happened in Argentina and throughout his career up to that point. He had been ringside for some of the most significant historical events of 20th-Century U.S.–Latin American relations, and he was eager to ponder these experiences at length. He looked forward to organizing his thoughts. The discipline and order of an academic life appealed to him, and he gave great attention to his lectures. He made himself available to both students and faculty there, and throughout the years he and Billy Ruth lived in Newport, he was in demand as a speaker on campus and elsewhere. He also wrote scholarly articles for political and military journals, including *The Annals of the American Academy of Political and Social Science* and *The Naval War College Review.*

Rick, shown here with his mother and sister, graduated from Phillips-Exeter Academy in 1963.

Recalling his time at the Naval War College, Dick says, "The Naval War College, like the Army War College, is for people who come there from all parts of government. I was assigned, as a representative of the State Department, to lecture and teach about Latin America. The Naval War College, of course, is under the Department of the Navy.

January 17, 1963. Ambassador Roy R. Rubottom, Jr., U.S. State Department Advisor at the Naval War College, presents one of his frequent briefings on foreign affairs to Naval War College staff and students.

Students come and stay for several months; there's housing on campus. So in a lecture class, I might have students from the military, FBI, State Department, CIA, or any other arm of the government. Topics of study included the history of war, for example, or U.S. involvement in international affairs. The student body is already past the mid-point in their careers, and this provides an opportunity for them to sit back and be students again, listen to lectures, travel. I enjoyed my time in Newport. The family was with me, and we lived right there on campus. In fact, the two biggest houses were for the War College commandant and for me, the State Department official. John, our youngest, was in school in Newport. Eleanor and Rick were away at school, but they were near enough to visit."

CHAPTER 13

Letters from the Field

During their peripatetic life in the service of the United States Department of State, the Rubottoms managed to remain closely tied to their families in Texas. Billy Ruth wrote reams of letters to her parents, to her sisters, and to old friends. Dick, too, wrote thoroughly detailed letters to his mother and sisters, as well as official letters to people in government, to academics, researchers, and to his counterparts in Latin America.

Today, these letters provide glimpses into the Rubottoms' life abroad. More than that, they amount to front-row seats to much of post-World War II United States history.

Dick's writing tends toward the academic, as he describes issues confronting the various players in U.S.–Latin-American relations. In his letters, he writes of his ideals, and examines the principles that he believes should guide a 20th-Century democracy.

Billy Ruth, by contrast, deals with the Rubottoms' daily life in her letters. As demonstrated in her description (in Chapter Four) of the virtual house arrest she experienced during the 1948 riots in Bogotá, Billy's purview is the home. But she also writes about the parties she and Dick attend, as well as the many times she is called on to be hostess. She describes what she wears, sometimes detailing how she managed to assemble an elegant outfit on a budget. Often she makes her own clothes, as well as clothes for the children. She discusses the family budget, or mentions her desire to lose a few pounds. She describes the stages the children are going through, and draws word-pictures of their clubs and school activities. She talks about being a Campfire Girls leader, or a Sunday School teacher. From her letters, the reader begins to comprehend the strength, creativity, and adaptability that a diplomat's wife and children must have if they are to thrive in this life.

What emerges from the Rubottoms' letters is a snapshot of a young couple from Texas, elegant, bright, and idealistic, who, despite the trappings and repeated relocations of the diplomatic corps, endeavor to provide a stable, rich, and normal life for their children.

Following, in chronological order, are excerpts from those letters home.

October 8, 1952, Billy from Washington, D.C., to her mother:

Just a note to let you know we are all getting along well. The baby is just precious—looks like Dick, I think. Weighed 7 lbs, 11 oz., and is getting along fine. I'm not going to nurse him, so they don't bring him to me but once a day. . . We named him John William.

November 7, 1952, Billy to Mary Jo:

Johnny is a wonderful baby and I'm having fun taking care of a tiny one again. He eats well—sleeps at night—and is a real pleasure.

We were certainly disappointed with the election—and truly surprised. From here we had the feeling Stevenson would carry many more states. I'm sure Eisenhower will make a fine President, and everything will be all right.

Do you plan to drive down from New York on Sunday, Dec. 14, or early Monday, Dec. 15? If you do stay in New York for church, go to hear Norman Vincent Peale at the Marble Collegiate Church. He is wonderful. We heard him in January when we were there. There is a possibility that Dr. Richmond may christen babies at our church that Sunday and we may have Johnny christened. We would like for you to be here for that, too, if possible.

I need to lose 12 or 15 lbs so you can imagine what a time I'm having with clothes. All this talk about it just dropping off is not working in my case so I'm going to have to work hard and get rid of it.

November 14, 1952, Billy to her mother:

The days do fly, and Johnny is growing. He weighs almost 10 lbs and is certainly a good baby.

September 18, 1953 from Billy Ruth in Madrid to "Dear Papa":

Ricky and Eleanor Ann start school on October 5. They have been busy the last few days getting ready for a play they gave yesterday afternoon. Their little club has 4 boys and 4 girls and they certainly do have a lot of fun together. They wrote and produced this play by themselves—sold tickets to all the parents and made quite a bit of money. Over $2 in all! I think they are undecided about how to spend it for charity. Ricky is interested in the Cub Scouts and is working hard on his achievements. Eleanor Ann is thrilled over our first meeting of the Camp Fire Girls, which we had here on Wednesday. There are about a dozen little girls 10 or 11 years old and they are going to have a lot of fun together.

Besides staying busy with the children, I spend lots of time trying to keep the house going. We have been trying to get a plumber to come for a week and he is here this morning and is going to have to tear up part of the floor downstairs. Madrid has had quite a drought and we have a water shortage, too. The main thing is the electricity shortage—we have four days a week without electricity from 4:00 a.m. until 7:30 p.m. The greatest inconvenience is Dick's electric shaver. Also the toaster and coffee maker. The rains are supposed to begin in October so we are hoping that it will be straightened out soon.

The children wear uniforms to school so I'm going to town with Eleanor Ann to try to get her outfitted this morning. I'll take Ricky another day.

Johnny is all over the place—pulling up and walking holding on but still not alone. He is fat and squeezable and we all enjoy playing with him.

Around Christmas 1953, a homesick Billy writing from Spain to her parents:

I've had a terribly frustrated feeling about so many things this year that it has been hard for me to get the Christmas spirit—but as the time approaches, the children seem to carry us along on their enthusiasm. Both the older children are really having a wonderful time planning for Johnny. I had a lot of fun watching them decorate our tree yesterday after church—and I wish you could have seen Johnny's face when he came in and saw it with the lights on.

I have been working hard this past week on a program of Christmas carols for the Campfire Girls and Cub Scouts—and we had it last night for 150 or 200 parents, friends, and brothers and sisters. The children were all in costume and acted out the story of Jesus. Eleanor Ann was an angel, and looked like one. Ricky looked darling and both of them sang so well.

At dancing class, Eleanor Ann turned her foot and it seemed to hurt a great deal and then it was all right. She complained once or twice the next week and then finally it hurt so much that we took her to the doctor. When he examined it, he said that it was a torn ligament and she would have to wear a cast for at least six weeks. She has been brave about it and doesn't complain too much—but it has cut her out of a lot and I'm sure it is not too comfortable.

Then Ricky had an accident, too. While I was at the doctor's office with Eleanor Ann, he had a basket of bricks fall on his head at the construction job next door . . . He had to have four stitches and his head was bandaged for more than a week.

We took some snapshots of them together just so we wouldn't forget this. I think we will send it next year and write, "This was our 1953 Xmas, and we hope yours is better than ours."

April 23, 1954, Billy, to her mother from Spain:

Ricky is back in school today—and at last we can breathe easily. He fell from the terrace to the garden (about 15 feet) and broke his arm just above the elbow on Monday, April 12. We have a very good bone specialist who has taken care of him for us—and we feel he has done a good job. The worry was caused by the lack of circulation the first night. I guess it is just as well that I didn't realize what the doctor meant when he told me that he couldn't feel any pulse. Ricky and I stayed in the hospital three days and he put a cast on it—finally—but told me it would have to be changed later. The final X-rays show that it is going to be all right.

October 9, 1955, Dick writing his mother. He refers here to a massive heart attack suffered by Eisenhower after 27 holes of golf on vacation in Denver in September that year. The public knew very little about the severity of this, but Dick, through the State Dept. was very sobered by the news.

[I have just returned from] a long trip around post-WWII Europe, where I have witnessed first-hand the damage from the war. I have been ruminating on the sacrifices our allies made in our common cause.

We are praying here for the full recovery of the President as we know you are. The first shock of his illness produced almost disbelief. Now we believe he is to survive to carry out this great purpose in which we know he has God's help.

The same week, Billy wrote to Frances:

One day a week I go to the Prado Museum for an art class—in Spanish—and I am enjoying it all so much. We are now studying Velazquez, and his paintings here are really marvelous.

Monday, October 28, 1957, Billy Ruth wrote her family from Washington:

We are going to the International Ball on November 8— I have a blue silk dress which I haven't worn yet. This is a charity ball which is supported by many wealthy people and is held the night before the opening of the Laurel Race Track, so there are lots of the "horsey" set. The raffle is fabulous. Last year Mrs. Edsel Ford won a mink stole—and she is contributing a new Edsel car to the drawing this year so I suppose one of the Rockefellers will win it. Anyway, we will be there to see all the fun. We are going with General and Mrs. Leavey (he is president of I.T.&T.) I still pinch myself that we see a lot of the people we read about in the paper.

We loved seeing the Queen—and Phillip. I think their visit here was a great success for everyone. No, Jo, Eleanor Ann didn't go to the Cathedral so you didn't see her on television. She and Ricky had a fever and watched it all on television here at home. They are fine and back in school now, but Johnny is at home with a cough. I don't believe any of them had the "flu" but everyone is being so careful now because there is so much of it going around.

By 1958, when Dick wrote this letter to his sister, the family was again living in Washington, D.C.:

I just heard the CBS World Roundup announce that the meeting of Latin-American Foreign Ministers beginning here tomorrow morning for two days will be "the most significant meeting in this hemisphere" ever held. That may be a slight exaggeration but it certainly is important enough to have kept me literally swamped with work ever since I returned from an all-too-brief outing in New York on the Tuesday after Labor Day. The meeting also comes at a time when Secretary Dulles is swamped with many other problems, as you well know from reading the newspapers, so an extra burden rests on the rest of us to try to help him as much as possible. I spent last Thursday and Friday in New York, hearing Secretary Dulles' speech, but mostly working in the corridors with the several Foreign Ministers who came up ahead of the meeting scheduled to begin tomorrow. In addition to the meetings for the two days, there will be a round of stag social activity, including a luncheon on Tuesday with President Eisenhower, a dinner at Anderson House by Secretary Dulles tomorrow night, and a luncheon at the Pan American Union on Wednesday as the final event.

The two older children started school last week. Ricky, in the seventh grade, has ninth grade textbooks for his English and his science.

Johnny started to school also, two weeks ago, and he is now beginning to go through the first pleasures of learning how to read.

Dick writing to his daughter, Eleanor, from his new posting in Argentina, on March 5, 1960:

Dear Eleanor,

We're now flying at 9,000 over San Julian, and we are due to land in 45 minutes at Rio Gallegos to refuel. The land was green for the first two or three hours after we left Buenos Aires this morning at daybreak, but since then it has been burnt and foreboding, almost as bad as the lifeless desert that stretches 2,000 miles down the West Coast of this continent, through Peru and Chile. By dusk or earlier we shall be at Rio Grande, on the north side of Tierra del Fuego (Land of Fire) where we shall spend two days at an estancia, fabulous when compared with its surroundings, owned by the wealthy Menendez Behety family.

Occasional farms or small ranch clusters stare up at us, even a few trees have been planted, but it is mostly miles of nothing but nothing—at least on the surface. Typical of the reviving Argentina is the oil drilling at Commodoro Rivadavia where we refueled at noon. The American families (Pan American Oil Company and Loab Rhodes) scarcely can find housing even at high prices typical [for] oil-boom conditions.

While waiting at Commodoro Rivadavia, a nice man named Mr. Bedford and [his] eight-year-old daughter introduced themselves. He is a Baptist missionary from New Mexico, whose wife is from Lubbock. When I told him I was born in Brownwood, he recalled Howard Payne College. He preaches to Americans of mixed denominations in English, but primarily ministers to the Argentine Baptist community. In two and one-half years he has won thirty-two converts, he said. It was English missionaries who first opened up Tierra del Fuego 120 years ago, the first group being slaughtered during a church service—but others followed.

The entire south of continental Argentina, known as Patagonia, was denied to European settlers for centuries. It was not until the "Campaign of the Desert," led by General Roca, and finally won in 1882, that the hostile Indians were overcome and settlers could begin to move in. Even so, development could have been faster had not Argentine citizens, including many European immigrants, chosen to stay in the cities. Many of them must have been seeking escape from their marginal lives on worn-out European soils, not realizing that the soil was Argentina's greatest wealth. Then Perón's drive to industrialize, at the cost of the farmer, drove more of the rural population into the cities, leading to a first-class problem today.

Our trip to Salta, one of the northernmost provincial capitals, on February 18-21, presented a different Argentina from that of today, at least on the surface. Salta was the main getaway, or one of them, to the Spanish colonies in Peru and Bolivia. The city is a Spanish colonial town, rich in history. We were there as guests to participate in the ceremonies commemorating the Battle of Salta, February 20, 1813, won by General Belgrano. His victory over the Spanish Royalists was one of the keys to the eventual independence of Argentina. The people are still proud of their achievements, their ladies are still beautiful in the Spanish way, yet they are ambitious and energetic, making one feel more confident of Argentina's future than one does residing in the capital.

Two highlights were: (1) The parade of the gauchos, dressed as they had 150 years ago when they won battles of harassment similar to how Mosby's Raiders did in our Civil War, and mounted on beautiful criollo (native) horses; (2) my handing to a well-groomed middle-class Argentine the title to his property (home) in a neat new housing development. In the latter event, the British, Soviet, and Turkish ambassadors also participated. In fact, the Soviet representative is a hard-working type. He speaks Spanish fairly well and has lived in Colombia (prior to its break with the Soviets in 1948) and Uruguay.

We came, we saw, and we *were* conquered. Arriving at

Rio Grande at 6:30 p.m., March 1, we were met by the Governor of Tierra del Fuego, Captain Campos (Argentine Navy, Retired), and others including Fernando and Marucha Menendez Behety. We drove to the latter's steam-heated home on the estancia named after his grandmother, Maria Behety. Our first surprise was the beautiful flowers, all colors and all varieties except tropical. They had a hothouse, but some were outside. Next we saw two guanacos, similar to vicuña or llama, playing by a pond. Enormous flocks of geese were everywhere, to the point of being pests. They are considered inedible here. But the main emphasis is on sheep, both for wool and meat. This is beautiful grazing country. Fortunes have been made from sheep. Our host showed us his prize rams being readied for the livestock show in Buenos Aires, known as the Palermo show, next August. On this place they concentrate on producing the corriedale variety of sheep, it reportedly being the best all-purpose breed for this climate.

We also visited the kennels where they raise their prize pure-blooded collies. The pure breed puppies are eventually turned over to the shepherds for use as sheep dogs and, of course, the blood strain eventually becomes diluted. We passed several herds of sheep (Piños) on the road en route to the slaughter house. They are marked with red paint on their backs, being selected on the basis of age, poor quality of wool, and other physical factors.

And now comes oil! Slightly more than a year ago, Tennessee Gas & Oil of Houston started drilling under its contract with YPF (Argentina State Oil Company) and it now has forty producing wells. Their success has far exceeded expectations. American families are here, and more are coming, although housing has to be provided. Tennessee Gas & Oil has twenty-five or more families. Then there are the subcontractors, also mostly American. I flew in a small plane over the field, then landed and drove to a pilot-type refinery just finished. It will produce enough gasoline and fuel oil to provide requirements of Tierra del Fuego.

At Rio Grande, the drilling sub-contractor, Laughlin-Porter, has arranged for two classes of the children of their American families to be taught by two American teachers in the regular public school building. They range from Grade 1 to Grade 8, so the teachers, as well as the students, must call on all of their resources to teach and to learn, much like the "Little Red Schoolhouse" of years past in the United States. I shook hands with each of these youngsters. Then I visited one of the classes of Argentine students. One immediate distinction: American students, when introduced, remained at their desks, while the young Argentines stood immediately when I entered, and in unison said, "Buenos Dias, Señor Embajador." The distinction doesn't really mean very much other than a different approach to schooling. In many Latin-American classes, there is still the learning by rote and reading aloud in unison. The American children were just as respectful but more relaxed.

The grumbling of big landowners is already audible—and much of it is directed toward the United States. But they'll get over this "phase" and many now realize that progress has its price. The Tennessee Oil manager, George Blackwell, is from central Texas. He worked near Brownwood, and later he was in Venezuela. He seems to have the knack of getting along with the Argentines and a sense of his big responsibility.

Our "private" hosts wanted us just to relax and enjoy ourselves. The second day, March 2 (Texas Independence Day), we planned to fish, and we did. But the weather was inhospitable, with overcast skies and intermittent rains, which could only mean cold. We drove across the pasture in an unbelievable Volkswagen "Combi" (literally, everything including the kitchen sink), and we wet our hooks in the Rio Grande. Soon our fingers were numb, and our feet, too, since we didn't have waders. All the warm clothes we bought were insufficient. Overlooking nothing, the hosts prepared an asado on the bank, and the fire helped. Back home we went again to fish for two hours, at a better spot, we hoped. But the fish didn't get the word for Billy and me. I landed a small trout and a big one got away when the line unknotted. Others, especially General Larkin (retired Lt. General heading a World Bank Transportation Mission to Argentina) did better, he catching two salmon of close to seven pounds each. Billy reeled in a two-pound brown trout hooked by our guide.

Fishing in Argentina is by a different standard than in the United States. Only the big ones are appreciated, but the small ones are more fun to reel in. In time, Billy and I could become devoted to the sport. It's relaxing. It imposes patience of which nobody ever has enough. That night we dined at 10:30, all of us exhausted and happy, with eyelids drooping throughout the five-course dinner.

On March 3, Friday, our "public" host took over, somewhat to the chagrin of others. (This is a problem for us everywhere here, not serious but latent. The private citizens are not always happy with, let alone of the same political persuasion with, the government people.) The visit to the oil fields lasted until noon. Then we flew for lunch to "Viamonte," the family estancia of Oliver Bridges, direct descendant of Thomas Bridges, first European settler in Tierra del Fuego, and relative of Lucas Bridges, author of the book *Uttermost Part of Earth*. His aunt Bertha, of numerous years, was a lively luncheon partner and has survived well her birth in Tierra del Fuego, the first white child born there. His wife is an American citizen who lived for many years in Mexico with her previous spouse. The Canadian ambassador was also there with his wife and 18-year old son, they being house guests. At the earliest possible hour, 4:00 p.m., the Governor, General Larkin, Harry

Conover (Economic Counselor of Embassy), and I "took off" in a British-built Land Rover for Ushuaia, 175 kilometers away. By good fortune and with an excellent driver, we arrived in five hours. The road was passable in most places, but a few spots were as bad as the Texas oil fields before pavement and after heavy rain. We had to use front and rear wheel drives with lowest gear to pull through. The need for a highway is real and urgent, since most of the oil field equipment has to come that route, Ushuaia having a fine port and Rio Grande almost no docking facility. Our knowledge of Tierra del Fuego topography and appreciation of its beauty were vastly enhanced by the overland trip, and this at no risk to our health, we hope. The first two hours took us through rolling sheep land marked by low trees and bushes. Then we skirted the eastern side of Lake Fanyano, a beautiful body of water 80 miles long, which extends into the Chilean portion of Tierra del Fuego and empties into the Pacific. We followed it on its southern side for nearly half its length, passing starkly denuded forest areas caused by an earthquake years ago. In spite of high hopes for tourism at the lake, it will be a hardy fisherman or sailor who will brave that beautiful but cold spot for fun. Too cold for swimming or water skiing. Hotels or lodges are still a dream to come, and I would vote for roads first if I had a voice.

Mountains were in view all day—this crooked extension of the Andes turns from its southerly plunge to run from west to east in Tierra del Fuego. In fact, the rainy cold we had on March 2 had produced snow in the mountains, even on the lower slopes. We were surprised to find the passes to be quite low—about 1,300 feet—in a range going up to 8,000 feet here. We drove through rain, sleet, and snow during the afternoon. The governor's family, some of his aides, and the Chilean Consul (Tomás Arizabal) met up at a paradoe (rest house) only 23 kilometers from Ushuaia. After coffee we drove on, to that windswept southernmost city in the world. We stayed at Government House, stark and simple but possessing "comforts." We had a pleasant dinner with the governor's handsome family—wife and three daughters named Maria (with suitable suffixes), their son being in medical school in Buenos Aires. We slept under four or five blankets with no windows open (and mind you, it is summer down here).

The maid who served us breakfast is Chilean, there being thousands of them working all over Patagonia (southern Argentina) and Tierra del Fuego. They seem to go and come freely without documentation. The young Chilean Consul took his Ph.D. from Woodrow Wilson School of Government at the University of Virginia and he had heard me speak on U. S.–Latin American Relations in Washington in 1957.

The governor took us "sightseeing" (it is lovely with the backdrop of snowy mountains and glaciers), also for a call on the Naval Base Commander, and finally for a little shopping. The fact that the city is a free port hardly compensates for the freights and, I suppose, profits that are reflected in the prices. I bought Billy some small scissors and myself a flat, stainless steel multi-purpose pocket knife. (Billy earlier had found some fleece-lined ankle boots in the Rio Grande, which saved her life during the fishing.)

At 11:00 a.m. we had the traditional "copa de vino," with nice exchanges of toasts, at Government House. The governor's wife and Conover went to meet our plane at 11:45, bringing back Billy, Lt. Col. and Mrs. Tally, and Major Kirkpatrick. The governor's wife then managed to serve a splendid buffet to about forty people in their small home. We had planned to depart in the plane for Rio Grande at 3:00 p.m., but we still had another surprise coming. During the morning, word came that President Frondizi and party were coming in the afternoon and the governor insisted that we stay to greet him—even though his plane didn't arrive until 5:10 p.m., thus delaying our take-off until 5:30.

Here I had to make a difficult decision. At first I couldn't believe the governor would want the United States Ambassador in his way when he had to attend to his president. The weather, in this case, couldn't have been better, so we could not fall back on the necessity for an earlier take-off for our 40-minute flight back to Rio Grande. But the governor insisted. I thought then that he didn't even have to tell us of the president's arrival, since it had been a well-guarded secret and we could easily have been gone by 2:30 or 3:00. Still, he insisted, and I finally decided he genuinely wanted us to stay. The governor has a highly developed sense of public relations. He had woven together a skein of ideas—the president, the ambassador, the oil boom with the United States companies doing the work, and all this converging in the "uttermost part of the earth." Not a bad thing! The president was certainly surprised to see us, but he was cordial, as always. He, too, seemed to catch the governor's enthusiasm, for after arriving at Estancia "Maria Behety" last night, we had a call that the president would fly over today (March 5) to visit Tennessee oil camps.

Last night was a splendid occasion. Good company, good cheer (inner and outer), fireside, good food, and lively discussion. Naturally, we touched on politics, but why shouldn't we? Our contributions were mostly questions to evoke reactions from our intelligent host and hostess, plus an occasional observation—constructive, we hope. They are responsible citizens. We pray that Argentina, and the United States, too, have enough of that kind. Over coffee, I had a thank-you statement that could not have come more from the heart. They deserved much more than words after such an outpouring of human warmth and generosity. We shall be seeing them more, we trust, and they'll come to know how sincere is our appreciation. Indeed, I think they sense it already.

Today, March 5, at noon, we're in flight to Buenos Aires, due to arrive at 6:30 p.m. We've missed church today, but we've received spiritual enrichment from our experiences and associations.

Love,
Dad

December 19, 1960, Billy Ruth writing to her mother in Texas:

Dear Mama,

Eleanor arrived safely last Wednesday . . . Ricky is due next Wednesday night. Tomorrow I am having a tea for the wife of the president, Señora Frondizi, and I've invited all the wives of the cabinet and the Supreme Court. I'm trying to get my Christmas decorations done for that.

January 19, 1962, Dick writing from the Naval War College to Ricky, who was away in boarding school:

Dear Ricky,

Your good letter came on schedule and made us happy with the news of recovery from cough, the basketball, the night study period, and the renewed determination. We are receiving two or three postcards per week from Eleanor Ann filled with news of her busy, joyous life . . .

I just climbed the stairs after watching a mixed 45 minutes of TV. First, an enjoyable, really first-class ice show from Switzerland; then the story of the war years of Robert E. Lee, an inspiring man.

Life is really that kind of mixture and we shouldn't forget it. Arnold Toynbee, the great historian, depicts history as a great series of ebbs and flows. I think there will be occasional setbacks for all of us to learn from, thence to progress to higher ground.

I find my own thinking regarding the state of our country to be an interesting fusion of ideas. On the one hand, the primary need is for spiritual dedication and renewal of religious faith—in our case, faith in Jesus Christ. Some have interpreted this Christian spirit as signifying nothing but continual turning of the other cheek and lying down before one's adversaries. I disagree. This week we have had some splendid lectures on modern naval weapons and tactics, and I find myself reassured by the knowledge. Especially that pertaining to the nuclear-powered submarines now armed with the Polaris missile.

Mother showed the car to me and told me of the bump. I'm glad the lesson was not a harder one—it reminded me of a couple I learned in Brownwood years ago, first on a friend's model-T and then on Aunt Lil's car.

Dec. 31, 1962
Dick writing to his mother and sisters from Newport

Ours has been a wonderful family Christmas, and we are sure our thoughts of you all have been joined with yours. Love erases distance and makes time stand still. If you were here, our second floor bedrooms and Ricky's attic room would be even more lived in, because the first floor, in spite of storm windows and a sturdy furnace, has the zero cold winds whistling through it. Our snow of pre-Christmas came and went quickly, but the gale of yesterday has brought us the coldest weather of our Newport experience. Before this the children had several days of good ice-skating on a large marsh nearby, and Sunday, Dec. 23, we had a day such as might have inspired Whittier or Longfellow or others of the New England school of poets. Good friends from Spain days, the Robert Bartons, and their three sons, invited us to join them in a cottage, good for summer and winter, on the edge of a large pond. The ice was solid so the children skated and played hockey. It was

only ninety minutes from here, so we drove up in time to
join them in a lovely old (but redecorated) Congregational
Church service before lunch, departing about 7:00 p.m. A
Spanish family known to us both, the father now Consul
General in Boston, joined us.

**This letter, written after the Rubottoms had decided to re-
turn to Texas, gives a thumbnail sketch of their finances
after a decade and a half in the State Department:**
April 29, 1964
Mr. Jack R. Young, President
State National Bank
Corsicana, Texas

Dear Jack,

Billy and I are happy to share with you and our other
friends the good news of our return to Texas about July 10,
when I shall become Vice-President for University Life at
S.M.U. We look back with gratitude on a 23-year span in
the Navy and Foreign Service, years of challenge and opportunity. We look ahead with excitement to the challenge at a
great university which is about to embark on its second
half-century.

We would appreciate the bank's assistance in making
this transition. I shall receive a lump-sum payment of
about $9,300 for my accumulated annual leave, less in-
come tax. We shall be settling accounts for purchase of
a new 1964 Rambler 770 station wagon, fully equipped
including air-conditioning, sometime in June, and will require $3,000 until such time as the net payment for leave
is received, probably about August 1. There may be other
expenses incidental to moving, although I trust not. The
main costs of moving will be defrayed by the government. Meanwhile, we shall be operating on a thin margin.
Which would you prefer—to send me a note which I could
sign and return if we need it, say in amount of $500, not

including the car, or would you like to have some other arrangement?

I shall be glad to inform you the details of our financial situation when I see you in July. In confidence I can say that my Foreign Service retirement annuity and salary will approximate $30,000 per annum. The equity in our house in Washington, say about $13,000, represents about half of our net worth. We do not yet know whether we shall sell it or retain it as a good investment. We shall have to look over the housing situation in Dallas before coming to a decision. With respect to our $2,600 loan at the Bank, we probably shall pay off most of it next summer after sizing up prospects or start retiring the debt on a regular basis subject to your agreement.

We look forward to hearing from you, and then to seeing you. We trust that all is well with you and your family, and with the bank.

Sincerely,
R. R. Rubottom, Jr.

Part Three

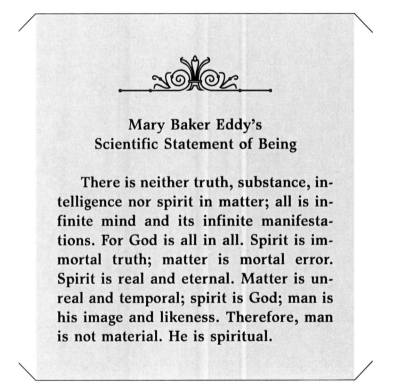

**Mary Baker Eddy's
Scientific Statement of Being**

There is neither truth, substance, intelligence nor spirit in matter; all is infinite mind and its infinite manifestations. For God is all in all. Spirit is immortal truth; matter is mortal error. Spirit is real and eternal. Matter is unreal and temporal; spirit is God; man is his image and likeness. Therefore, man is not material. He is spiritual.

CHAPTER 14

Homecoming

On November 22, 1963, while the Rubottoms were living in Newport, President John F. Kennedy was assassinated in Dallas. This tragic moment in history led to deep nationwide grief and anxiety, and also required countless behind-the-scenes adaptations by government workers and officials. And without question a Johnson administration would spell change, Dick understood, for his own diplomatic career. Why?

Several years earlier, when Dick was Assistant Secretary of State for Inter-American Affairs, and LBJ was Senate Majority Leader, Johnson had wanted to take a trip to several South American countries that had problematic relations with the United States. The State Department advised against such a trip, and someone—allegedly in Rubottom's department—leaked this caution to the press. The trip was cancelled.

Incensed, LBJ sent over an associate, who demanded to know who had leaked the information. Rubottom didn't know, nor did he feel it appropriate to launch an investigation into the matter. It was a small matter, actually; certainly no national security had been compromised. But Johnson became furious and held it against Rubottom from then on. So it was a given: Roy Richard Rubottom, Jr., would not be appointed Ambassador again as long as Johnson was in office.

Therefore the time had come for Dick, in conversation with Billy Ruth and a few close friends, to begin reassessing his options.

First of all, he knew he would not take a lesser position in the State Department. After reaching the rank of Ambassador, any other appointment would be unacceptable.

Having settled that, Rubottom considered the idea of international consulting, and he corresponded with several friends and colleagues about it. He had in mind consulting for leaders in Latin-American business and government, where he had so many contacts and such extensive experience. But the reports he received from friends who were doing this work made clear that it would take years for him to establish a stable client list, and that money would be tight until then. Rubottom was 52 years old; he had three children to educate. So the idea of consulting went no further.

And anyway, there was another professional dream that had never left Rubottom, that of his first (and intended) career, the one he'd just begun when the war intervened: he wanted to be in academia. Whether as administrator or teacher, he wanted to be on a first-rate college campus.

At the same time, Dick's old friend and college roommate, Willis Tate, had been president of Southern Methodist University in Dallas since 1954. Tate was highly respected, an effective, far-sighted leader for Rubottom's beloved alma mater. Rubottom had always kept close ties with S.M.U., and when Willis Tate heard that Dick might be leaving the State Department, he invited him to return to Dallas as Vice-President.

With that, Dick decided to retire from the State Department and move back to Texas with Billy Ruth and

John, now age eleven. This would be their twenty-fourth move in twenty-five years.

Here is the citation awarded Rubottom on the occasion of his retirement:

Department of State

UNITED STATES OF AMERICA

to

Roy Richard Rubottom, Jr.

on your retirement from the Foreign Service it is my privilege to express to you the appreciation of the Government of the United States for the

Loyal and Meritorious Service

which you have rendered your country In your career of 22 years devoted to the interests of the American people you have earned the gratitude and respect of your Government.

Done at the city of Washington this 31st day of August in the year of Our Lord One Thousand Nine Hundred and Sixty-Four.

Dean Rusk

Secretary of State

Rubottom's official retirement certificate

The back of the citation read:

RRR Jr., a Foreign Service Officer with the rank of Career Minister, was appointed a Foreign Service Officer of the United States on May 3, 1947.

He served abroad as Second Secretary and Consul at Bogotá; First Secretary and Consul at Madrid; also Economic Counselor and Detailed as Deputy Chief and later Director of USOM to Spain; Ambassador Extraordinary and Plenipotentiary to Argentina.

While in the United States he served with the Department of State as Officer in Charge of Mexican Affairs, Office of Middle American Affairs; Deputy Director and Director, Office of Middle American Affairs, Bureau of Inter-American Affairs; Deputy Assistant Secretary and Assistant Secretary for Inter-American Affairs; detailed as Faculty Adviser, Naval War College.

Mr. Rubottom received a Superior Service Award in 1952.

He was appointed a Career Minister in 1962.

Date of Retirement
August 31, 1964

Certificate from President Kennedy awarding Rubottom the rank of Career Minister, the highest rank in the Foreign Service.

CHAPTER 15

S.M.U.

Dick Rubottom always held that his life had been significantly shaped by his time at Southern Methodist University. Only sixteen years old when he arrived as a freshman, he'd spent five years in college and graduate school there. He had excellent teachers, and he made life-long friendships. He looked forward to being back on campus when he returned, as Vice-President for University Life, in time for the 1964-65 school year. He'd be an administrator, but he hoped he would also be able to teach and lecture, perhaps in the Political Science Department.

But something happened before they moved to Texas that took the Rubottoms by surprise: they learned that Dick's coming to S.M.U. was controversial in Dallas. Very controversial.

The head of S.M.U. Public Relations at the time was a man named Marshall Terry, who vividly recalls the brouhaha around Dick's hiring. "There were editorials, and the Dallas papers took up the subject, casting doubt on Dick's character," Marshall says. "People on campus already knew Dick as a friend of Willis Tate's, but when he was invited to work at S.M.U., local conservatives immediately trumpeted that Dick had praised Castro at a certain point in his State Department career. Dick had said Castro

221

was a Robin Hood or something. Later, of course, when Castro became a genuine Communist, Dick was the first to acknowledge it."

But in the spring of 1964, when the John Birch Society got wind of Rubottom's appointment, they started an "information campaign" through which they advised the public that Roy Richard Rubottom, Jr., was a left-wing radical. By way of demonstrations, angry letters to regional editors, and flyers attached to car windshields, they stepped forward to voice their opposition to his coming.

But where had they gotten the idea that Rubottom, an Eisenhower Republican, was a Communist? A columnist for the *Richardson* (Texas) *Digest*, Earl Lively, fired the opening salvo when he wrote, on May 6, 1964, "Conservatives who [have] long been critical of the liberal atmosphere of Southern Methodist University can get some consolation from the recent hiring of Roy Rubottom, Jr., by the university. While Mr. Rubottom brings a way-out liberal philosophy to the job of S.M.U. Vice-President for University Life, the school's stewards have done the nation a great service by hiring him away from the State Department."

Lively went on to accuse Rubottom of being "responsible for the policy which forced Batista out of Cuba so that Castro could take over."

A few days later, a critical article concerning Mr. Rubottom appeared in Philadelphia, in a publication called *Eastern Banker*. Two months after that, in July, a two-page anonymous letter was mailed to S.M.U. students and parents in the Dallas area, with a return address of "Student Advisory Committee" and a post office box number. Around the same time, an article titled "Southern Methodist University Pampers Leftism," by Harold Lord Varney, was placed on the windshield of the S.M.U. librarian and additional copies were mailed to key university supporters.

S.M.U. Vice-President Keith Baker was charged with apprising Rubottom, who was still in Newport, of these attacks. He wrote Rubottom a letter outlining the above communications, and in a letter dated July 15, 1964, Rubottom replied:

> Thank you very much for conveying the information contained in your letter of July 10, and for calling me on the phone on July 13. Even though the material used by the anonymous vilifiers is old and comes from some discredited sources like Nathaniel Weyl and Batista himself, I realize that it cannot be swept under the rug. The university cannot fail to take it seriously any more than I can. The way we try to deal with this problem depends ultimately on whether the campaign against me (and against the university) continues, and whether it spreads.

The attacks, of course, came from a misunderstanding of events during the period in the 1950s before Castro had allied with the Soviet Union. During that time, Rubottom had cautioned against labeling Castro a Communist and thus pushing him over to the Soviets. Rubottom's extensive research indicated that Castro wasn't ideological when he first came to power, and Dick believed there was a chance that the United States, by not shutting the door to Castro and his increasingly successful revolution, might influence Castro toward a more democratic Cuba.

"At that point," Rubottom explains, "it was just too soon to label him, and I said so. Later, of course, Castro started his anti-American tirades and it became clear that he had made his stand as a Marxist or Communist."

He shrugs and gives a rueful smile. "But I guess my not being ready to jump in and immediately pigeonhole him made me a Castro-lover to certain people in Dallas."

Rubottom's position on that point was clearly substantiated by a memo from Former Secretary of State Christian Herter to the Associated Press and United Press International. Herter had received word of the attacks on Rubottom, and on November 29, 1962, he formally responded:

> My attention has been called to recent press reports . . . in which the integrity of former Assistant Secretary of State Roy R. Rubottom, Jr., is impugned.
>
> I understand that charges are also made that the foreign policy of the United States in regard to the Cuba question was made at lower levels of the State Department.
>
> Mr. Rubottom was a close associate of mine for a number of years while I served as Under Secretary and as Secretary of State, and I have the highest regard for his patriotism, integrity and skill as a Foreign Service Officer. This judgment, I believe, is shared by his contemporaries in the Foreign Service and other high-level officers in the administration of President Eisenhower who had occasion to work with him.
>
> The idea that important foreign policy decisions were made at levels other than the highest in the State Department is a patent absurdity. Under my administration of the State Department, the able staff of the department was fully used, but important decisions in all cases were taken only with the highest authority of the State Department.

What the protestors apparently didn't realize in approaching S.M.U. President Willis Tate with their complaints was that Tate was a fervent champion of free speech. In fact, a few years earlier, Willis had been written up as a Communist himself, by none other than H. L. Hunt. This came about because some S.M.U. students had invited John Gates, editor of *The Daily Worker*, to speak on campus. Vociferous criticism erupted at the idea of having a known Communist at S.M.U., but Tate, in the interest of free speech, stood behind the students' invitation.

"John Gates did come to campus to speak," Marshall

Terry says, "and, I might add, not too many students were converted to Communism."

Terry goes on to recall another controversy from the same period. A theologian named Shubert Ogden was on the faculty of Perkins School of Theology at S.M.U., having come there from Yale. After Ogden published a book called *Christ Without Myth*, Marshall says, "People interpreted Ogden's book as saying that Christ was a myth, so Ogden was *persona non grata* among conservatives. It's hard to imagine that a university would be attacked for books in its library and speakers on campus, but S.M.U. was attacked for exactly that. On the subject of free speech, we had made our stand even before Dick arrived."

From the outset Willis Tate stood firm in defense of Rubottom's fundamental integrity and evenhandedness, and he had no patience with those who called on him to renege on the invitation to his old friend. In a memo to faculty and administration about what had become known as "The Rubottom Matter," President Tate wrote, in part:

> 1. We will take the position that Rubottom is a superior appointment with ability, training, and experience that will greatly strengthen the University. His appointment is not open to consideration, but is a fact in which the administration takes pride.
> 2. We deplore the anonymous attempt at character assassination, and we are sick that there are those who live among us who will stoop to such.

Then he outlined a plan of action in which he encouraged his fellows, among other things, not to panic or lose faith that truth and justice would prevail; not to go on the defensive; and to find out who was behind this smear campaign. He promised to prepare a two-page, carefully worded and dignified reply to send to people who wrote in, and he ended by writing, "Let's get on with important work as soon as possible."

Perhaps for that reason, by the time the Rubottoms settled into their new home on Wentwood Street, the hubbub

Back at S.M.U., Rubottom enjoyed working with his old friend and college roommate, Willis Tate, now S.M.U. president.

had largely died down. It was decades, in fact, before John Rubottom, who moved to Dallas with his parents, even learned of the hate campaign against his father.

The Rubottoms give great credit for this to Willis Tate and his steadfast support.

"Dick immediately became very active in Dallas," says Marshall Terry, "and in no time he had overcome people's prejudices about how 'far left' he was. He was very popular. The faculty liked him, and students did, too. He and Billy Ruth were highly stylized as a couple, and very formal. They always observed protocol. It was just an attitude he had: inclusive, but serious."

Terry reports that Dick quickly became a part of S.M.U. leadership. "Willis had a cabinet, which I was on," Marshall recalls, "and Dick was made a part of that inner circle. As to leadership, I really loved Willis Tate. He was like a father to me. However, Willis was not good at delegating. For that reason, it was helpful to have someone like Dick on board, someone who was a scholar and also highly organized. I remember he always carried a yellow pad around; he called it his 'tickler list.' We all came to rely on Dick. We had had a provost for a while, but no administrative Vice-President, so Dick became that, in effect, which helped Willis a lot.

"Dick was also an adjunct professor in political science, and he taught and lectured as much as he could."

Marshall describes Dick during those years as one of the stalwarts of the university. "Philosophically, he was very important," Marshall says. "I knew him in two main ways. I was director of S.M.U. Public Relations, and as such I was assistant to Willis Tate. This meant that I also worked with Dick on day-to-day administrative issues. Too, I worked with him during the Master Plan period."

Asked to elaborate, Terry says, "About halfway through Willis Tate's tenure, a committee of fifty business leaders,

alumnae, and friends of S.M.U. spent a whole year planning for the future of the university. I was charged with
writing a master plan on the basis of the studies we made.
Dick was on that committee, and he was the most influential voice for a strong liberal arts orientation. This was before Dick and Billy Ruth moved back to Dallas. He was
serving on the committee as an alumnus while he was still
at the Naval War College.

"Those meetings constituted the first time we had artic-
ulated our educational philosophy. The plan was supposed
to lead to a financial campaign. We were to get a large grant
from the Ford Foundation. However, that funding stalled because of our religious affiliation. But even without the funding, the study was helpful. Through it, we determined that
S.M.U. would have selective admissions, wouldn't grow all
that much, and would be stronger in research."

Willis Tate, in a letter to the Rubottoms on the occasion
of their fiftieth wedding anniversary, recalled how he
counted on Dick for support during the years of their leadership at SMU. He wrote, "You became my right hand as
Vice-President for Administration. The troubled days of in-
tegration and student unrest made it nice to have a diplomat around. You became indispensable to the political science department, teaching classes in Latin American
Affairs. Your continued research led you to be the regional
authority on international relations and to co-author a
book, with Carter Murphy, on U.S. contributions to modern
Spain." According to Dr. James Brooks, then Provost at
SMU, it fell to Rubottom to function as president of the university during a months-long sabbatical that President Tate
took during those years.

Brooks goes on to remember, "During the late 1960s
there was widespread student unrest on campuses across
the U.S. Thanks to the integrity and leadership of President
Willis Tate, Dick Rubottom, and those who worked with

them, SMU avoided the worst of these problems. One of the actions that helped SMU through this time came from Tate and his Executive Committee—certainly including Dick. Tate called for a study of the governance structure. This required an enormous number of meetings, especially with student leaders. These meetings led to the recommendation and ultimate implementation of a very inclusive plan that really touched essentially all of the University. But throughout and in the ongoing governance structure students were involved so that they had a legitimate and well defined role through which their input could be heard and their concerns addressed. Dick and I and others in the University administration sat through innumerable hours of meetings— first in addressing the need and then in implementing the plan that had been crafted. Those hours spent in the numerous meetings of boards, councils, etc., of course, represented time that normally would have gone towards fulfilling the 'regular responsibilities' of our jobs. Dick must have felt this. I know I did. But I would guess that, in hindsight, both of us would recognize the fact that it was a good and the right thing to have done. SMU came through that difficult time stronger and better positioned to move forward than did many universities. This accomplishment was a compliment not only to Tate but to Dick and others in the Tate administration."

CHAPTER 16

Building Community

When they moved back to Dallas, Billy Ruth and Dick saw the family more frequently. Dick's sister Nancy Merle and her family lived in Dallas, which made family get-togethers a regular occurrence. A few years later, Dick's other sister, Martha Frances, moved to Dallas to live with Nancy Merle, which meant the Rubottoms had the opportunity to spend more time with her as well. Young family reunions met at the Stagecoach Inn in Salado, Texas, from 1980 on, every year. And they enjoyed going to Ruidoso, New Mexico, for bridge weekends with relatives Maurice and Eleanor, Anna Mae and George, Tillie Frances (whose husband, Fred Nagle, had died), and Mary Jo and Lewis.

And another connection grew out of Rubottom's participation in the S.M.U. planning committee. Dr. James Brooks, professor of geology, also served on that committee. He later became Dick's close friend and esteemed colleague.

Says Brooks, "I met Dick before he officially came to work at S.M.U. The university went through its master-planning process around 1960-61, and we had a prestigious, blue-ribbon external committee that included a number of university presidents, officials, alums, and others who had some interest in S.M.U. At the time, I was chair-

*Once they moved to Dallas, the Rubottoms enjoyed short "bridge hand va-
cations" with Billy Ruth's siblings and their spouses. Here in 1966, they
pose in Estes Park, Colorado. Front row, George Eliot, Lewis and Mary Jo
David, Eleanor Young, Billy Ruth; Back row, Dick, Anna Mae Eliot,
Maurice Young.*

man of the Department of Geological Sciences, but I was
also very involved in long-range planning for the university.
Like so many others, I was very impressed with Dick and
Billy Ruth, and delighted when he came aboard as Vice-
President in 1964."

Dr. Brooks says that, while Rubottom originally came
back as Vice-President for University Life, he quickly out-
grew that title. "I recall that his title was soon changed to
Vice-President of Executive Affairs or Executive Vice-
President. He had a lot of responsibility in administration
of the university. In fact, after Willis had been president for
a number of years, he got a grant for senior university officials who needed a rest from long, unbroken service. It was
some foundation's way of giving officials a sabbatical with-

out the university's having to pay for it. Back then, universities didn't have sabbaticals for administrative personnel. Anyway, Willis was on leave for six months or a year in the late 1960s, and Dick was, in effect, interim president during that time. Of course I worked with him even more then, and I got to know him well."

At the end of the 1968-69 school year, Dr. Brooks assumed the joint title of Associate Provost and Dean of the College of Liberal Arts. "The Rubottoms and we became great friends," he says. "We socialized a good bit."

He chuckles as he remembers something. "As I'm sure you know, Dick was very active in scouting. At one point there was a scouting program called Hands Across the Border, an adult scout leaders conference that took place every spring. One year it would be held in the states, and the next in Mexico. Well, on this particular year it was planned to be in Moralia, Mexico. Dick asked me, 'Are you going? I don't mind driving but I'll need someone to navigate.'

"So my wife and I went with Dick and Billy Ruth, and I have to tell you, that was one of the toughest drives I ever made in my life. It was extremely harried. The roads were narrow and winding, and mostly overtaken by big trucks. We were all thankful just to make it to Moralia alive. And we were so tired when we got there!"

Undeterred, the Brookses and the Rubottoms made several more trips together over the years. "Besides Mexico, we also went to Guatemala and we took several trips together in the states, mainly doing scouting work. Dick and Billy were excellent traveling companions."

Recently, Rubottom was asked whether it had been hard to make the transition from the diplomat's life to the quieter academic life. "We adjusted quickly," he replied. "We were in a welcoming community. Willis Tate was my closest friend and former roommate and fraternity brother. Billy

Ruth was close to her family. The fact is, she made every adjustment quickly. She could easily have been spoiled, but she wasn't. She stepped into her new life without a problem. She was adaptable, versatile, gracious. People were drawn to her. For a man in my two careers of diplomacy and university administration, I couldn't have had a better partner than my wife Billy Ruth."

These qualities were captured in the following profile of Billy Ruth that ran in the *Dallas Morning News* soon after the Rubottoms' return.

Embassy Wife Finds Service Abroad Preparation for Life

The Dallas Morning News
by Mary Brinkerhoff
August 26, 1964

Billy Ruth Rubottom, now returning to campus life, never finished college. Living and learning among foreign peoples, she put credits on her country's record, not her own.

Mrs. Roy Richard Rubottom, Jr., wife of a new S.M.U. vice-president and U.S. Foreign Service veteran, wouldn't have had it any other way. You couldn't get her to trade for the years in Mexico, Paraguay, Colombia, Spain and Argentina—or for those in Washington.

THE GIRL FROM Corsicana and the boy from Brownwood shared a career during which he rose to the rank of assistant secretary of state for inter-American affairs.

"In so many areas of our life," Billy Ruth feels, "the wife doesn't have to speak up or know anything about her husband's business. But in foreign service, the wife also represents the United States."

Some may hold that wives enjoy (if that's the word) a like

responsibility in shaping the public's view of the academic world where the Rubottoms first teamed up and where they are getting established again.

Dick is already on the job as S.M.U. vice-president for university life. Before long, the Rubottoms hope, they will have acquired a Dallas address of their own.

MEANWHILE, they are grateful to vacationing friends, Mr. and Mrs. M. M. Miller, for the loan of their comfortable home at 3824 Shenandoah.

John, born nearly 12 years ago in Washington, was there with his mother when a reporter came to visit.

Not yet transplanted to Dallas were Eleanor Ann, 22, who will be a senior this fall at Pembroke College in Providence, R.I., and Rick, 19, a prospective University of Texas freshman. Rick's birthplace was Asuncion, Paraguay; his sister was born in Corsicana.

All speak Spanish, like their parents. Mrs. Rubottom says, in fact, that the youngsters have learned, forgotten, and relearned the language several times.

BILLY RUTH YOUNG first met her future husband, who holds two S.M.U. degrees, when he was assistant dean of student life and a graduate student at the University of Texas. She was an undergraduate working as a secretary in the president's office across the hall.

After World War II Navy duty, during which he served in Mexico and Paraguay, and a term as a Corsicana banker, Dick joined the Foreign Service.

There followed duty at the U.S. embassy in Bogotá, Colombia; a period in Washington during which he rose to be Director of Middle American Affairs; assignment to Spain, with eventual rank as head of the U.S. mission for economic aid, and return to Washington.

Dick served longer than anyone else had, his wife recalls, in the hot-spot job with responsibility for inter-American affairs. He next became ambassador to Argentina. He came to

S.M.U. from a post as State Department adviser at the Naval War College in Newport, R.I.

ALONG THE WAY, the Rubottoms weathered an army coup in Paraguay, rioting in Colombia and the occasional criticism which all foreign service career men expect.

But these are not the things that Billy Ruth Rubottom remembers in conversation.

She's inclined, rather, to talk about what might be called foreign service at the human level: friendships with people from all walks of life, church and welfare work, travel to remote areas, culture exchange.

And she's a great believer in such unofficial contacts. "Our government has a definite job to do, but all these other facets of our life go abroad too."

In Argentina, her husband used to organize round table sessions involving different groups—labor, professional, student—and often mixing antagonistic factions. "Some would talk together in the presence of the American ambassador when they wouldn't speak to each other anywhere else."

Embassy wives took a course in the host country's culture, along with another designed to prepare them for answering questions about their own.

ONE ARGENTINE episode made the Texans feel they had never left home. In 1961, they were on hand for the 125th-anniversary celebration of the First Methodist Church of Buenos Aires. So was Bishop Umberto Babieri, who held three degrees from S.M.U.

Mrs. Rubottom is delighted to be settling down with her family as a part of Dallas and the S.M.U. community, "hoping to stay in one place for a while."

Yet she feels that the years abroad have given her children a priceless preparation for life on a shrinking, changing earth. "So often, we become educated people without knowing about the rest of the world."

Dr. Brooks points out that Dick was very influential in the Boy Scouts of America. "He received local, regional, national, and international recognition," Dr. Brooks says. "He has been awarded all of Scouting's most prestigious awards to adults for exceptional leadership: the Silver Beaver, the Silver Buffalo, and the Silver Antelope. Very few people are so honored, but Dick certainly deserved it, because he did so much to spread support of scouting."

---

8 September 1984

Resolution of the International Committee Boy Scouts of America

Every group, local, national and international, that has had the good fortune to number R. RICHARD RUBOTTOM among its members or supporters has caught the fire of his dedication to and work in the service of peace, understanding, and goodwill among all people.

Scouting throughout the Americas has immensely benefited because of his wise counsel and dedicated toil during the years he served as a member of the Committee of the Inter-American Region, World Organization of the Scout Movement.

The resolution is unanimously adopted to record the International Committee's profound respect and high regard for R. RICHARD RUBOTTOM. The International Director is hereby commissioned to spread the resolution across the records of the International Committee, and the Internationals Commissioner is directed to deliver a suitable replica of it into the bonds of this consecrated Christian and devoted American.

E. F. Reid, International Commissioner

Attested by: G. Jay Heim, Director

International Division, BSA

Now that he was back on a college campus, Dick had the opportunity to make a leadership contribution to his old fraternity, Lambda Chi Alpha. As noted in a 1972 profile of Dick in the official Lambda Chi publication, *Cross and Crescent*, his return to S.M.U. ". . . was a rich opportunity to serve, not only higher education but also the fraternity system so instrumental in Dick's early career."

The article went on to say that Rubottom had arrived at S.M.U. "at the very moment when analytical minds and courageous voices were needed to guide an increasingly defensive fraternity system throughout the continent into channels more in focus with the modern issues prevalent on campuses."

During the 1968 Lambda Chi General Assembly meeting in Dallas, Dick was elected to the Grand High Zeta, the ultimate honor bestowed by the fraternity. He continued there from 1968–1976. As a member of the board of directors of the fraternity's educational foundation, he served as secretary, vice-president, and president. Throughout these years, he called for leadership, integrity and involvement on the part of fraternity members. "Yours is the chance," he said in accepting his award, "to provide the fresher voice, the clearer words, and the more impelling and credible leadership."

Rubottom wanted, in other words, for new fraternity members to experience the inspiration and brotherhood that he had at their age. He had honed his natural leadership skills while a college student, he knew, and Lambda Chi had been a big part of that.

He continued to hold leadership positions in the fraternity until his late seventies.

Dick was a member of the Rotary Club of Dallas, and he served two terms as president: in the 1970s,

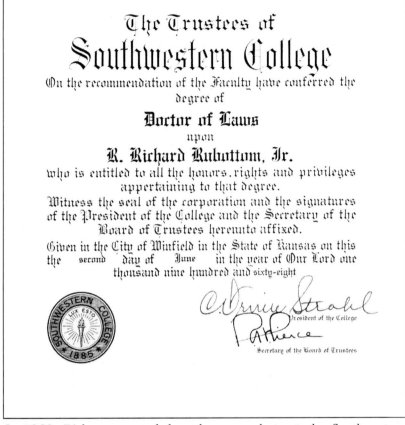

In 1968, Dick was awarded an honorary doctorate by Southwestern College in Winfield, Kansas.

and again in 1994-95. He remained interested in international and educational programs, to which he gave energetic support.Through Rotary, Dick forged additional alliances and friendships, and his sphere of influence continued to widen. He liked to encourage others, especially younger people, to become involved in Rotary, and he had a keen eye for people with leadership qualities. Raul Aguilar was one such person.

Raul says, "Dick was always after me to join Rotary and in 1988 I did join the Rotary Club of Dallas. Part of my reasoning was that it would give me a chance to spend more time with him."

Dick and Raul met originally through an elite ethics committee on which they both served. Recalls Raul, "In 1980, the State of Texas opened up the attorney review complaint process so that non-attorneys could participate. Eight attorneys and six non-attorneys were appointed by the State Bar Association, because of each individual's presence and influence in the community. Before moving to Texas, I'd served in a similar capacity in Minnesota, which was one of the first states to do this kind of work.

"When I moved to Texas in 1980, the president of the State Bar Association in Minnesota called the president of the Texas State Bar and said, 'Look if he's willing, you should get Raul involved, because he has a lot of experience in this area.' So I was appointed to the Grievance Committee for the 6th District of the State of Texas, which is the northern part of the state. Dick was on the committee as well, and I met him there.

"Those meetings could get intense and argumentative, because the grievance committee had subpoena powers, and we could prosecute attorneys for misdeeds. The attorneys on the committee wanted to stick up for the attorneys, and the laypeople were looking for justice. If lawyers were found innocent, fine, but if in the wrong, the range of punishments went from a slap on the wrist all the way to disbarment. Dick and I served together there for about six years, during which time we had to do all the discovery work, prosecution, evaluation of complaints, examining testimony, and so forth. It was complex, and a major time commitment. The process has changed now, but that's the way it was then.

"Through that work Dick and I became friends. In the process of hearing grievances, one's values and character became evident. Either you liked a person or you learned to dislike him or her. Dick was always the voice of reason, maybe because of his State Department experience. In any case, his was the calming voice when attorneys and non-attorneys got into heated discussions about the defendant's honesty or dishonesty. We civilians were representatives of society; the attorneys, the tops in their field, were there to represent the profession. They were the best of the best from the D.A.'s office, or top-flight practicing lawyers from well-known firms. A term was two years by appointment, with no more than three consecutive terms. Dick and I served the full six years, which were the formative years on the committee. I like to think we helped with establishing procedure. I know Dick did."

As soon as they arrived in Dallas, the Rubottoms joined Highland Park United Methodist Church. HPUMC was a well-established church, having held its first service, as University UMC, back in 1916. A year or so later, the congregation moved to Highland Park, where the church stands today, a white brick building of uncommon grace on Mockingbird Lane. The grand sanctuary of this 12,000-member church was where the Rubottoms could be found every Sunday morning for decades.

They faithfully attended the "Mr. and Mrs." class for married couples, and served as co-presidents in 1979-80. Dick did several lectures series at the church. One, in 1968, was a four-week course titled "Our Latin-American Neighbors." Dick served as Chairman of the Administrative Board, was named to several North Texas Conference boards, and completed two terms as a member of the Pastor-Parish Relations Committee.

While Dick participated in the Convocation on Religion and Race at Dallas' First United Methodist Church in 1988, and the 1990 Cross-Roads Project of the Greater

From *The Tower*, November 12, 1993, in acknowledgement of Billy Ruth's having been named "Volunteer of the Month":

Billy Rubottom interested in missions; Volunteers to help keep archive records.

When Highland Park United Methodist Church's Volunteer of the Month for September joined the church, she obviously took quite seriously her pledge to uphold the church through her service. Billy Ruth (Mrs. Richard) Rubottom has been a very strong supporter of Highland Park and has been active in many different aspects of church life, including the Missions and Church Resources Work Areas, [as well as in] the United Methodist Women. She never misses a UMW meeting, and she has been a key participant in Highland Park's support of both the Bethlehem Center and the bridge-building efforts with Hamilton Park UMC. Also, she has been a tireless supporter of the church library.

Archivist Jessamine Younger knew about Billy's deep level of involvement in the church when she spoke to a group about needing someone to spend some time entering data into the archives' computer. She said that she couldn't believe it when Billy raised her hand and said, "I can do that!"

And for the past two years, Billy has indeed done that. She has come in once a week, for two to three hours at a time, to add, delete, and combine records of the archives. As Jessamine explained, this is very detailed, exacting and important work. The church archive is the repository of documents that have enduring value to the history and heritage of Highland Park United Methodist Church. And having an index of these documents is vital to being able to actually use the materials.

Billy, your work has been invaluable in setting up and maintaining this index, and Highland Park United Methodist Church would like to take this opportunity to say, for your work in the archives and for everything else you have done, a very grateful "Thank You!"

Billy Ruth and Dick often traveled with Herb and Kay Miller. Herb was Dick's first cousin on his father's side.

At a family reunion in Salado, Billy Ruth poses with her siblings. Left to right: Maurice Young, Anna Mae Eliot, Billy Ruth, Tillie Frances Nagle, Mary Jo David.

Dallas Community of Churches, Billy Ruth served on the Church Resources committee, joined a women's circle, and spent many hours volunteering at Bethlehem Center, located in a high-poverty area of Dallas. They both taught Sunday School.

That Convocation on Religion and Race proved inspirational for Dick, in large part because of a speech delivered there by Bishop Bruce Blake. Titled "Visions of Inclusiveness," it addressed the need for more interracial and inter-ethnic dialogue. Two years later, as an associate lay leader in his local church, Dick helped forge a coalition between HPUMC, a largely white congregation, and Hamilton Park UMC, a predominantly African-American church east of Central Expressway.

Working with a committee of members from both churches, Dick helped initiate what was called "bridge-building dialogue." It started with lunch and conversation in the Great Hall of the church and evolved into monthly meetings. By the following year, members of the two churches were planning annual celebratory banquets.

The participants did more than talk, though. They formed joint Bible Study groups and worked together on repairs for elderly people without resources.

In an interview with Jerry Burford for the HPUMC newsletter, Dick said, "My wife has been such a wonderful help to me. She's the one who keeps me going. We never stopped worshiping God whenever we were stationed abroad."

But Highland Park Methodist Church, the Rubottoms had come to realize, was something different. It would be a new home.

CHAPTER 17

An Accident

Starting at age nine in Newport, John Rubottom became interested in competitive swimming, and by the time he was in high school he began to distinguish himself in the sport. The family encouraged him in this, and Dick and Billy Ruth enjoyed accompanying their youngest son to meets.

One weekend in August 1969, they drove John to the National AAU Long Course Championship meet in Louisville, Kentucky, where he was to compete in the 1500-meter freestyle. In the car with John and his parents were Eleanor and her husband, Allan Odden. The couple had gotten married on May 28, 1966, in Perkins Chapel on the S.M.U. campus. The Oddens, both teachers in New York City, were spending the summer in Dallas, and they decided to join Eleanor's parents and younger brother, John, on the trip to Louisville.

At the end of the meet, the family stayed to watch the finals of the Sunday events. When the competition was over, they all piled into the car and started their drive home, aiming to make it to Memphis for the night. Dick and John rode in the front seat, and Billy Ruth, Eleanor and Allan were in back. It was late. The roads were dark, and it began to rain.

244

Suddenly on that dark Kentucky highway, just over a small hill, the Rubottoms' car slammed at full speed into an 18-wheel flatbed truck that had been abandoned in the middle of the road. There were no lights or flares to mark its presence, so nobody saw the impact coming. This was a time before required use of seat belts—and there were none in the back seat anyway—so everyone was jammed forward, slammed back, then pulled and jerked every which direction.

Billy Ruth, from her place in back, wound up face down on the floor with a broken shoulder. Eleanor, sitting beside her mother, broke her left tibia and ankle. John, shotgun, broke his right femur. Amazingly, Allan was unhurt.

By far the most extensive injuries were Dick's. His spinal column was damaged, and he had eighteen fractured bones, three of which were compound fractures. He broke both shoulders as well as both feet and ankles. He couldn't move.

Allan got out of the car to direct traffic, and a passerby called an ambulance. The family was rushed to the nearest emergency room, which was located in Elizabethtown. With everyone injured or stunned into silence, Allan made the necessary decisions and functioned as a liaison between the family and the doctors.

But Dick's injuries were myriad, and so serious that many local medical facilities would be unequipped to address them. As it happened, though, this Central Kentucky county seat had on staff two excellent surgeons, who had done their orthopedic residencies at Belleview Hospital in New York City. This was more than fortuitous, because Dick's broken body had to be treated with great care. Helping his skeleton knit back together would require skill and patience. For starters, he was kept immobile in the Elizabethtown Hospital for six weeks.

As soon as Rubottom could be moved, William

Clements, then Chairman of the Board of Trustees of S.M.U., sent a plane to transport him home to Texas. Dick was strapped into a sandwich stretcher, which rendered him completely motionless throughout the trip.

Back in Dallas, he was admitted to Presbyterian Hospital, where he remained for more than four months, spending day and night in a Stryker Frame. This is a device made of canvas stretched on anterior and posterior frames. With a Stryker, the patient can be rotated around his longitudinal axis. This keeps his blood moving, but the patient is not moving his body at all. When the doctors looked at Dick in the Stryker they shook their heads in doubt that he would ever walk again.

But he did walk again. In fact, long months of rigorous rehabilitation meant that Dick, after a year and a half, returned to robust good health. He credits this, in large part, to swimming, an exercise he found highly therapeutic. He says little of the discipline and sheer will his healing must have required.

As it happened, Dick and Billy Ruth had started a renovation of their one-story ranch style house on University Boulevard even before the accident. They had added a swimming pool, a third bedroom, and a carport at the back. They also updated the dining room and kitchen.

The pool had fiberglass siding, which created a year-round greenhouse. All the children remember the beautiful orchids and amaryllis, as well as hanging ferns and hibiscus, that Billy Ruth grew in the pool area.

Billy Ruth also devoted considerable time to needlepoint. "She made beautiful pillows and Christmas stockings," Eleanor says. "She taught me how to needlepoint in the early 1970s. She was a loyal member of a University Women's group called the Knit-wits."

In addition, Billy was an accomplished gardener. She tilled a vegetable garden in the back yard beyond the pool, and there she grew asparagus, squash, and tomatoes. She became a dedicated composter long before it was in vogue. John remembers watching her sift the dirt and separate out the finest for her garden.

After the accident all of the changes in the Rubottoms' house seemed fortuitous, as Eleanor observes. "Dad had to have intensive physical therapy when he got home from the hospital, so he swam every day in that pool, from the time he was allowed to swim after the accident until they moved out of that house many years later."

By the end of 1970, only sixteen months after the accident, Dick was able to walk to his office on campus.

There were few long-term effects of the accident. Dick had always had good posture, and the only hint of his injuries was that his erectness perhaps increased, and seemed more studied. Billy Ruth considered it miraculous that her husband bounced back as he did. She and his many friends saw it as testament to Rubottom's tenacity, courage, and grit.

Asked today what he understands of the near-miracle of his healing, Dick says, "I have always tried to be a positive thinker. While I was trying to get strong again after the accident, I repeated the three affirmations. They helped me heal."

CHAPTER 18

New Horizons

The Rubottoms had settled easily into their life in Dallas. For many reasons the city felt familiar to them. Dick liked teaching and enjoyed being back on the S.M.U. campus. They had scores of friends, both old and new. They were socially prominent in the city, and they continued to entertain often, while also attending countless philanthropic, church, and college events. They kept season tickets to the Dallas symphony.

Two years after the accident, Dick was offered the position of President of the University of the Americas in Puebla, Mexico. He decided to take the job, and he and Billy Ruth moved to Puebla in 1971, remaining there until 1973. Among others attending his inauguration as president of the university was Dick's old friend, Willis Tate, who later observed, "I was amazed that the inauguration was conducted completely in Spanish, and further that Dick could climb the stairs so soon after his traumatic family automobile accident."

During his tenure at University of the Americas, Dick established an Industrial Advisory Committee to assist the school of technology. He also restored the university's relations with the Jenkins Foundation, which contributed about $1 million to university operations during his time there.

The Rubottoms at the luncheon following his inauguration as President of the University of the Americas.

As President of the University of the Americas in Puebla, Mexico, the Rubottoms hosted countless formal functions. 1971.

Earlier, U. of A. had lost its accreditation, and while president, Dick led the school through the rigorous process to official reaccreditation. He also helped the university acquire a building in Mexico City, which doubled its plant size. To pay for renovation, he obtained $5 million in A.I.D. [U.S. Agency for International Development] funds. And finally, he found the funding to staff the Inter-American Business Center at the university.

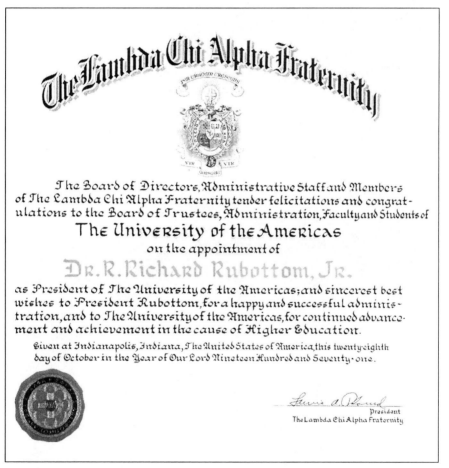

The Lambda Chi Alpha Fraternity

The Board of Directors, Administrative Staff and Members of The Lambda Chi Alpha Fraternity tender felicitations and congratulations to the Board of Trustees, Administration, Faculty and Students of

The University of the Americas
on the appointment of

Dr. R. Richard Rubottom, Jr.

as President of The University of the Americas; and sincerest best wishes to President Rubottom, for a happy and successful administration, and to The University of the Americas, for continued advancement and achievement in the cause of Higher Education.

Given at Indianapolis, Indiana, The United States of America, this twenty-eighth day of October in the Year of Our Lord Nineteen Hundred and Seventy-one.

President
The Lambda Chi Alpha Fraternity

Rubottom's fraternity, Lambda Chi Alpha, congratulated him on his appointment as President of the University of the Americas.

Dick's sister, Nancy Merle, visited the Rubottoms in Puebla.

When he was Assistant Secretary of State, Dick's secretary had been Beth Beers, whom he later recruited to accompany him to the University of the Americas. A career foreign service secretary, she recalls that time in Mexico as a learning experience. "I knew nothing about universities so had much to learn and found it fascinating to observe the many ways in which the Rubottoms effectively contributed to the development of the U. of A. and won new friends and supporters for it in the Puebla region," she says. Beers especially cited meetings of the Rotary Clubs in Puebla (where the university was located) and in Cholula (where the Rubottoms lived), as well as Billy's volunteer work with handicapped children and the Rubottoms' entertaining of local industry, business and professional leaders.

This was a productive time for the University of the Americas, but at the end of his second year, Dick and Billy Ruth were both ready to return to Dallas—and they did just that in 1973.

Having reached retirement age, the Rubottoms remained busy and influential. Dick had retired from the administration staff of S.M.U., but he continued to teach and lecture. The family was growing, and Dick and Billy Ruth took great pleasure in their children and grandchildren.

Adding to the shelf-full of awards Dick had already received—Superior Service by Department of State 1952; Citation by the National Civil Service League 1958; S.M.U. Distinguished Alumnus 1958; the Silver Beaver Award from the Boy Scouts of America in 1976—new awards and commendations continued to come his way. In 1991, he received the H. Neil Mallon Award for Distinguished Civic Service given by the Dallas Council on World Affairs, and in 1993 the Silver Buffalo award from the Boy Scouts of America.

As professor emeritus at S.M.U. he was in wide demand as a speaker, notably for the World Affairs Council of Dallas as well as chapters in other cities. From 1979 to 1982, he was foreign relations adviser to former Gov. William P. Clements.

Additionally, he was on the Good Neighbor Commission of Texas from 1981-87, and served as its chairman in 1982. He was president of the Board of Directors of the Owens Foundation from 1983-87 and served on the Steering Committee of the Aspen Institute Project on Western Hemisphere Governance from 1980-88.

His interest in immigration led him to accept a position as a public member of the State Bar Association Immigration Committee, where he served for more than a decade. As mentioned earlier, he served six years on the Grievance Committee for the Texas State Bar Association 6th District in the 1980s.

Dick always enjoyed his work.

Dick and Billy Ruth loved to travel, so in Fall 1979, Dick accepted a position as Diplomat in Residence of World Cruise, Semester at Sea. In that capacity, the couple boarded a big cruise ship along with 400 college students, and set out to see the world. Known as University Afloat, the ship traveled around the world in roughly a hundred days, starting from San Francisco and ending in Fort Lauderdale, visiting world capitals and remote villages all along the way. Dick lectured on Latin America, and he and Billy Ruth enjoyed seeing the world's cities as tourists and academics rather than as representatives of the United States government. This kind of travel was both relaxing and enlightening, a delightful break from routine for both of them.

The Rubottoms spent six months aboard ship in 1979 when Dick was named Diplomat in Residence of World Cruise, Semester at Sea.

As for the family . . .

Eleanor's husband, Allan Odden, was a Professor of Education Leadership and Policy Analysis. Eleanor, meanwhile, had earned a doctorate in Learning Disabilities from Teachers College, Columbia University. In the early 1980s, the Oddens lived in Denver, Colorado, where Eleanor was Coordinator of Reading for Jefferson County Schools. Their daughter—the Rubottoms' first grandchild—was born in Denver on May 1, 1980, and named Sarina Elizabeth.

On November 25, 1984, Robert Allan Myung Soo Odden was born on Cheju Island, Korea. He was adopted by the Odden family in November 1986 while they were living in Los Angeles.

For his part, Rick was beginning a long and highly suc-

The family gathered for reunions every year in Salado. This picture was taken in 1986.

cessful career in quality assurance. His work dealt with the American manufacturing sector. In 1993, Rick was recruited to work in Houston at the Westinghouse Turbine Repair Center. He resides in Houston today.

John, the youngest, married Lynn Thompson in 1973, in a wedding at Highland Park United Methodist Church in Dallas. He graduated from law school in 1979, and in the early 1980s worked as an associate attorney at McCall, Parkhurst & Horton law firm. In April 1981, John and Lynn had a son named John William Rubottom, Jr. They called him Jay.

John moved to Austin in 1988, so that John could set up an Austin office for his law firm. The next year, in 1989, he took a job with the Lower Colorado River Authority [LCRA]. In December 2007, John became General Counsel for LCRA.

After John's move to Austin, his first marriage ended, and on December 22, 1990, he married Angela Jane Taylor in a ceremony at University United Methodist Church in Austin. Their daughter, Taylor Elizabeth, was born the next year.

With that, Billy Ruth and Dick Rubottom had four grandchildren, and they surrounded themselves with photographs of their children and grandchildren for the rest of their days.

The Rubottoms' grandson, Robert, became a U.S. citizen in 1987. Here he is shown with his sister, Sarina, and Dick and Billy Ruth.

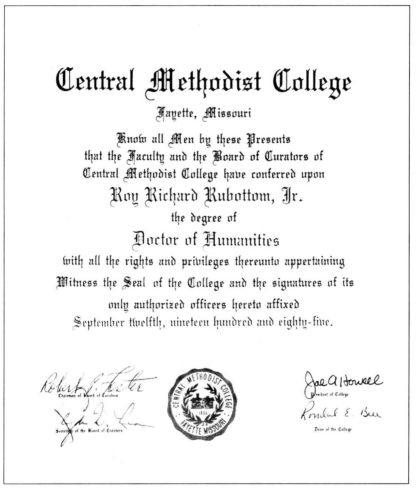

Central Methodist College

Fayette, Missouri

Know all Men by these Presents
that the Faculty and the Board of Curators of
Central Methodist College have conferred upon

Roy Richard Rubottom, Jr.

the degree of

Doctor of Humanities

with all the rights and privileges thereunto appertaining

Witness the Seal of the College and the signatures of its

only authorized officers hereto affixed

September twelfth, nineteen hundred and eighty-five.

A second honorary doctorate was awarded to Rubottom by Central Methodist College, in Fayette, Missouri, in 1985.

CHAPTER 19

Bringing the World to Dallas

(Dallas Office of International Affairs)

In 1984, when he was in his early seventies, Dick Rubottom was tapped for the job of Director of the Dallas Office of International Affairs. This office, which had been created in 1981 by the Dallas City Council, had formerly been called the Office of Protocol. However, by 1984, the Protocol office was under-funded and under-staffed, and its director, discouraged, resigned.

Dick was approached about the job, and he was interested—but only on his own terms. The following article appeared in the *Dallas Morning News* on September 2, 1985.

Dallas Tends to Protocol:
Officials Redouble Worldlier Pursuits
by Chris Kelley

In April 1984, the Dallas Office of Protocol was in chaos, and Dallas' quest to be known as a world-class city appeared to be seriously off course.

The city's first chief of protocol, a former career diplomat named Darrell Carter, had recently announced his resignation in a harsh letter to city officials.

In the correspondence, Carter said the 3½-year-old office was "an orphan, a stepchild" that received little support from the City Council of city management and was hampered by interference from outside "interest groups."

Unless the city corrected serious problems within the department, the Office of Protocol would be "doomed," said Carter, a former U.S. Information Agency employee.

Seventeen months later, city officials say the renamed Dallas Office of International Affairs—led by a strapping 73-year old former ambassador to Argentina—is back on course with a significantly enhanced status and expanded mission.

Created by a skeptical City Council in August 1981 to coordinate the visits of foreign diplomats, the Office of Protocol was funded during its first year by a $36,000 budget provided by the Dallas Chamber of Commerce and the Junior League of Dallas.

The office had a professional staff of two that had to rely on hundreds of volunteers to handle a steadily increasing number of visiting foreign dignitaries. Its role was limited almost solely to "official" ceremonial greetings.

During its first year of operation, the protocol office—later moved from the fourth floor of City Hall to a corner of the lobby, much to Carter's chagrin—handled 78 "official" visits from foreign dignitaries.

Carter reported to a city department head and rarely dealt directly with City Manager Charles Anderson or Mayor Starke Taylor.

Today, the Office of International Affairs has a professional staff of four, an annual tax-supported budget of $102,000 and a major role in seeking foreign trade. The office is coordinating a foreign trade mission that Taylor will lead to Japan in mid-September.

By the end of next month, the office will have handled more than 1,000 "official" foreign visitors to City Hall since October 1984, officials said, and soon will be moved to the fifth floor, where it will have direct access to Taylor, his staff and conference room.

The office's new director, R. Richard Rubottom, Jr., reports directly to Anderson.

"We learned a lot from those early days," Anderson said. "We were bootstrapping ourselves into the international affairs arena, and Carter helped us do that and pointed out what we needed to do more of.

"But we had to prove ourselves with small steps before we started taking larger steps, as we're now doing with Dick Rubottom, who has the skill and the vision to make a giant leap forward into the bigger international arena," Anderson said. Anderson appointed Rubottom to direct the office in April after a national search. Rubottom was with the U.S. State Department for 17 years, which included stints as assistant secretary for Inter-American Affairs and as ambassador to Argentina under President Eisenhower. He returned to Dallas in 1964, and served as both an administrator and professor at Southern Methodist University before retiring in 1977.

In addition to coordinating ceremonial visits—with the help of the Dallas Chamber, the Dallas Committee on Foreign Visitors and the Dallas Council on World Affairs—Rubottom said he spends considerable time planning and promoting international trade.

His message to foreign dignitaries: "Dallas will be a respected, important city, not just because of its airport, or its banks, or its industries, or the World Trade Mart. It will be a city of international outreach to the extent that Dallas is a city that provides opportunity to its own citizens and solves its own problems and deals with its own minority groups and provides them with opportunities equal to the so-called majority."

Anderson said Rubottom will accelerate the city's efforts to become well-known abroad.

"If we are truly committed to becoming an international city of prominence, we must have a more effective Office of International Affairs, and Dick Rubottom will make that happen," Anderson said. "He has brought intelligence, insight and energy to the office...and with his level of competence—coupled with our commitment to elevate the importance and the accessibility of the office—we will become that city."

When Dick became international director, he found an old student of his working in the office, and he was delighted to renew that acquaintance. Lolis Longoria (now Dignan) had come in right after Darrell Carter resigned as Chief of Protocol.

Lolis well remembers the day Dick arrived on the scene. "Dr. Rubottom had been one of my professors at S.M.U. in the middle 1970s. He was my Latin American politics professor, and he was also the chair of the department where I got my degree—the Ibero American Civilization Depart-

In 1984, at age 73, Dick was named Director of the Office of International Affairs for the city of Dallas.

ment. I only went to S.M.U. for a year, as a transfer student, and Dr. Rubottom was one of the best teachers I'd ever met. He brought personal experience to the subject of Latin American politics. He was able to talk about some of the people in our books because he had met them. It was fascinating. He was humble, too. I remember when the class entered, he wrote his name on the board and said we could call him by his first name. Of course nobody dared. But he was very approachable.

"After meeting him when I was a student, I didn't see him again until he came to the international office. The whole department was in disarray when Dr. Rubottom came, and he brought dignity and order to the office. His mandate was to build a de facto foreign affairs department for Dallas, to provide support and advice to the mayor and city council on matters of protocol, and to be able to provide appropriate hospitality to dignities visiting from other countries. Dallas had many international visitors."

Dignan explains that Rubottom's position and responsibilities evolved over time. "We did international business, protocol, sister cities, etc. I had come in prior to his arrival in a kind of keep-'em-together capacity, as Interim Chief of Protocol. When Dr. Rubottom was hired, he asked me to stay, I guess as his first assistant. He brought such statesmanship to the office, and such presence. He had all the qualities you would expect a former ambassador to have."

Sharon DeGarmo was also working in the office when Dick arrived. She explains that the international office was funded, in part, by the Junior League of Dallas, and it was staffed by 25-30 Junior League volunteers. "They brought China, stemware, flatware, and other things to entertain with," she says. "They also funded my position, which was Special Events Coordinator/Volunteer Coordinator."

DeGarmo, too, recalls the shape of the office prior to

Dick's arrival. "When I first came, they had installed as Acting Director a young man with a Naval background and no relevant experience. After he quit, the Junior League chair, who was from a prominent Dallas family, took over for a while. But the job kept growing. Positions changed hands and changed hands until Dick came in and brought order to the office. He was already 73 years of age, but he was debonair, very tall, striking and well-dressed. He was also a great dancer."

Lolis Dignan agrees. "Certainly Dr. Rubottom brought sophistication and grace to the office. It just came naturally. He was highly respected by all of us, and by other city workers as well."

In Dallas with Dick's sister Nancy Merle.

Both women recall that hundreds of visitors in those years were drawn to the city by the television series *Dallas*. Says Dignan, "Almost everybody who came from other countries wanted to know about that T.V. program. Dallas—meaning the city itself—got a lot of free publicity from it. People were intrigued by those fictional characters, and we were the beneficiaries. South Fork, where the program was filmed, was actually a working ranch and by the early 1980s it was a for-profit venue. We had events out there."

One especially memorable event during Dick's tenure was the visit of Prince Charles of Great Britain. This was a very big occasion in Dallas, and the Office of International Affairs spent four months planning for it.

"Prince Charles came without Diana," Sharon remembers. "We were all disappointed at that. The Prince's trip was a good will trip arranged through the British Consulate here, by a Consul named David Hollamby. Charles was on

WHERE: Southfork ranch.
WHEN: April 11.
WHAT: More than 20 ambassadors, in Dallas for the next night's Mayor's International Ball, were treated to a barbecue and country music.

In 1986, the Rubottoms planned a barbecue for visiting ambassadors and dignitaries.

his way to Washington and he came through Dallas at Hollamby's invitation.

"We arranged to have the Kilgore Rangerettes perform for him outside City Hall. They were to provide the Texas Welcome. However, Dick decided it was inappropriate for the girls to kick up their legs. He just couldn't imagine allowing that kind of immodesty in front of a prince, so he had them just bow and take off their hats. It was cute, but it's hard to imagine the Rangerettes not doing their kicks. Prince Charles was intrigued and went over to talk with them.

"Afterward, the Consul was inside waiting to greet him, but Prince Charles was so busy visiting with the girls that he didn't come in at the appointed time. When he finally did enter, we all stood and turned to him. We hosted a buffet in the international room, a large room with flags of all the consulates in Dallas."

During those years, the Office of International Affairs launched a tradition called "Dallas World Salute," during which all the various ethnic groups in Dallas were honored through carefully arranged events. At the same time, Rubottom was active in the Consular Corps of Dallas and the World Affairs Council of Dallas, as well as the Council on Foreign Relations.

"He attended countless meetings," DeGarmo recalls, "and he kept up a massive correspondence. He was an excellent writer. Various people would write in and request information, or request introductions. He was always busy, advising the city, arranging protocol for royal and other international visitors."

DeGarmo chuckles as she remembers an incident that illustrates Rubottom's high standards. "Once we issued an invitation and it wound up with an extra apostrophe in the word *it's*, making it a contraction instead of the possessive. I remember the volunteers all had to take X-acto knives to the invitations and painstakingly scrape off that apostrophe. Dick was very precise. He had certain principles and levels of expectation, so it was very important that we do everything right. And of course that was required anyway, because of the nature of the office."

Rubottom did have one hard and fast rule around the office, says DeGarmo. "He always said, 'Never put anything negative in writing.' He told us he had learned that by working with Richard Nixon. Something that Dr. Rubottom had written for Mr. Nixon had been misconstrued, I think."

Sharon and Lolis agree that the office became more formal after Rubottom's arrival, but they emphasize that that was a welcome development to everyone concerned. "Everyone in the office called Dick Dr. Rubottom," Sharon recalls. "Volunteers and staff—everyone called him that, even though we had called all of our other directors by their first names. We knew he didn't have an earned doctorate, but it was a term of respect. When we would write his name, it would be Ambassador Rubottom. We always called his wife Mrs. Rubottom as well.

"All of us were impressed by their marriage. They made marriage look romantic, even in their seventies. We could tell they idolized each other. Both Lolis and I were divorced, and we found it so refreshing to observe their love. The volunteers, too, were taken by their regard for each other. We thought they exemplified what a good marriage should be."

Lolis agrees. "They were such a team. It was a true love story."

After a little less than two years, Rubottom resigned from the position. "His commitment to the people who recruited him was that he would get the office launched, and stay long enough to get it going," explains Lolis. "As soon as things were running smoothly, he went on to other pursuits."

Please join in celebrating

the Fiftieth Wedding Anniversary of

Billy and Dick Rubottom

Wednesday, December 21, 1988

four to six in the afternoon

Highland Park United Methodist Church

Activities Building
Mockingbird and Hillcrest
Dallas, Texas

John and Lynn Rubottom
Rick and Gale Rubottom
Eleanor and Allan Odden

In 1988, the Rubottoms celebrated their 50th wedding anniversary.

Dick and Billy Ruth cut the wedding cake at their anniversary party.

Following is a letter that Dick wrote to Billy Ruth on their 53rd anniversary:

December 22, 1991

Dearest Billy,

On the eve of our 53rd Anniversary, I still wonder how I could have been so fortunate as to be your husband.

Many of the joyous experiences stand out and we shan't forget the pain of others. Fortunately, we seem to have selective memories so the joyous drive out the painful.

The family had a formal portrait made for the 50th anniversary celebration. (Front row, left to right: Sarina Odden, Robert Odden, Jay Rubottom. Middle row: Allan Odden, Billy Ruth Rubottom, Dick Rubottom, Rick Rubottom. Standing: Eleanor Odden, John Rubottom, Lynn Rubottom, Gale Rubottom.)

Hardly a day passes that we don't recall something that was exciting, or fun, or significant, perhaps even lasting. Who knows? We might even have made a difference here and there.

One thing I know for sure. Without you, I could not have accomplished much or been as happy as I have. You are the love of my life and I am grateful for what you do to make me happy. And you are a wonderful mother and grandmother. Happy anniversary!!

With all my love,
Dick

Dick and Billy Ruth were co-chairs of the 1988 Dallas World Salute. Here, Dallas mayor Annette Strauss presents them with an award for outstanding service.

The Rubottoms chat with Senator John Tower at a Dallas event.

83. Always active in leadership of the Boy Scouts of America, Dick accompanied a group of Scouts to Santiago, Chile, where he arranged a visit with the U.S. Ambassador.

At a family reunion in Salado. Front row: Billy Ruth, Dick, Taylor Rubottom, Marilyn Primeaux. Standing: Sarina, John, Angie Rubottom, Rick, Eleanor, Jay Rubottom.

The prestigious H. Neil Mallon Award is presented by the Dallas World Affairs Council to an individual who has excelled at promoting the international focus of the Dallas/Fort Worth Metroplex. The award is presented here by Ann Mallon.

In 1993, Dick was awarded the Silver Buffalo Award.

The family in Dallas.

With President George H. W. Bush

*At a
Boy Scout
dinner
in1993.*

Part Four

The 23rd Psalm
The King James version

The Lord is my Shepherd, I shall not want. He maketh me to lie down in green pastures. He leadeth me beside the still waters. He restoreth my soul. He leadeth me in paths of righteousness for his name's sake. Yea, though I walk through the valley of the shadow of death, I will fear no evil, for thou art with me. Thy rod and thy staff, they comfort me. Thou preparest a table before me in the presence of my enemies. Thou anointest my head with oil. My cup runneth over. Surely goodness and mercy shall follow me all the days of my life, and I will dwell in the House of the Lord forever.

CHAPTER 20

A Journey in Faith

Throughout their seventies and most of their eighties, the Rubottoms participated in myriad intellectual and social activities. An example of their schedule is seen in one of the joint letters they regularly sent their children. In one dated February 24, 1998, Dick began, as he often did, with a Scripture reference. "And what does the Lord require of you but to do justice, love kindness, and walk humbly with your God?"

Then he wrote, "Lest you think our minds are not challenged, a look at last week's activities reveals just how fortunate we are."

He went on to list a fine lecture by Renee Prieto, S.M.U. professor of art history, who spoke on El Greco's "The Death of Count Orgaz." That was Monday. On Wednesday he and Billy Ruth heard a lecture on Winston Churchill by Professor Jim Hopkins, a widely respected professor of modern British history. Thursday the Rubottoms were invited to the Dallas Women's Club to hear Franklin Murphy, Supreme Court reporter for the *Washington Times*, speak on recent Court rulings and their implications for the country. Friday brought a noon talk by Ambassador Bill Richardson on Saddam Hussein's challenge to UNSCOM inspections and related subjects. On Sunday, of course, the Rubottoms attended services at Highland Park United Methodist Church.

For decades, the Rubottoms sent a Thanksgiving letter to many dozens of old friends. Originally typing on a typewriter, Billy Ruth became computer literate, after which, until the final letter was sent in 2000, she used the computer to print the letter and the mailing labels. These Thanksgiving letters caught their friends up the Rubottoms' travels, their children, the Dallas symphony, their plans for the coming year.

And invariably the letters concluded with a word of gratitude for the present and hope for the future.

During these years, the Rubottoms managed to stay in their house, taking care of themselves and living independently. They enjoyed their garden, their heated indoor pool, and especially appreciated having their children and grandchildren visit. One tradition Dick began was having all the grandchildren help him fill the bird feeder in the Rubottoms' back yard, and then watching as the birds came to sample the food.

Eventually, however, the inevitable advance of age made it necessary for them to sell their home and move to The Forum, an elegant retirement home on an oak-lined street in Dallas. The sprawling red-brick facility, with its white-columned portico, provided a comfortable apartment for the two of them in the independent living section, where they spent six active years.

Then they moved to an assisted living apartment for a year before determining that the time had come for them to move closer to at least one of their children. By this time, Eleanor and Allan were living in Madison, Wisconsin, and Rick was in Houston, so the family decided moving to Austin, where John, Angie, and Taylor lived, would be the best plan.

These are the formal photographs taken of Dick and . . .   *. . . Billy Ruth when they moved into The Forum. 1999.*

In the late spring of 2006, Dick and Billy Ruth moved to the Summit at Lakeway, a tasteful retirement home on the outskirts of Austin.

In January 2008, Billy Ruth died. When friends expressed their condolences to Dick, his reply was quick and rarely varied. "Billy Ruth and I had sixty-nine years together. Sixty-nine years!" He would shake his head in wonder at the blessing of so much time with her. "I could never have asked for a better wife. She was exemplary. She was a full and absolute partner to me."

He would look away and say, "I miss her, but I'm very grateful. . ."

At times in the months following Billy Ruth's death, Dick could be found sitting in his chair, apparently lost in thought. If asked, he would admit that he was repeating, in the deepest silence of his mind, the three affirmations that he is confident have carried him through his years.

Although he wears it lightly, Dick has a deep Christian

faith. It would be difficult to overestimate the role his faith has played in his life and work.

In July 1999, he was asked by his home church, Highland Park United Methodist, to give a talk about his faith. He accepted the challenge, attempting to put the ineffable into words in a talk he called "My Journey in Faith." In it he reflects on many of his life experiences as seen through the prism of his personal faith, and with the wisdom of many years:

My earliest memories—all bad—are of getting dressed for Sunday School. Bad not because of Sunday School, but because I had to wear a blue serge suit and a shirt with a detachable Buster Brown collar. The Sunday routine in our home was set in concrete; no deviation from both Sunday School and church. That is not surprising since both my grandfathers were Baptist preachers—on the conservative side.

I joined the church in Wichita Falls, Texas, when I was 9 years old, perhaps a little early to claim that I accepted Jesus Christ as my savior. It was, however, an emotional experience during a Revival where, legend has it, the renowned George W. Pruett of First Baptist Church, Dallas, was preaching. I remember quite well being baptized by total immersion in a baptistery behind the choir loft.

My boyhood Sunday School experience became a serious endeavor. My teacher was a highly respected dentist, Dr. Shelton, who was part of a distinguished family with deep connections to Howard Payne College. He was outstanding; he was one of two or three men who became father figures to me during those crucial fours years, age 12 to 16, while I was in grades 8 to 11.

My parents, Jennie Eleanor Watkins Rubottom, and Roy Richard Rubottom moved from Kingsville to Wichita Falls, and later, when I was ten, to Pittsburgh, Pennsylvania. Although we children were not privy to our parents' problems, they became so acute that my mother left Pittsburgh with the three children when I was 12 and returned to Brownwood where her parents and four married sisters resided. My father's limited financial support of the family ended in a year or two, and my mother operated a boarding house so as to survive and be independent during the remainder of my high school and university years. This was the end of my parents' marriage, although my father did not seek a divorce for years. I worked at an assortment of jobs all during my high school years.

This detailed account is important because it was a testing time for my faith, both in God and in myself. My mother was a stronghold of faith, never giving up, and always encouraging me even in the most parlous times. My faith in her was matched by her faith in me. My education, no matter how limited the resources, was paramount. Dr. Shelton, in Sunday School, and several of my high school teachers always had faith in me, as did the men under whom I worked in grocery stores, and many odd jobs. My aunts and uncles, and my maternal grandparents, W. D. and Martha Watkins, stood firmly behind me, although they could not render financial assistance. While money was in short supply, we had wealth in the resources that really counted, most of all an abiding Christian faith.

It was during those hard years that my mother turned to Christian Science. Her first steps were somewhat halting, but she eventually became a stalwart believer, as did my two sisters. I never became a Christian Scientist, but I respected that faith, observing what it had done for and meant to my mother.

In May 1928, I graduated from high school and accepted a tuition scholarship to enter S.M.U. There is no doubt that my mother's faith in me sustained me in crucial moments, even though I might have been unaware of the presence of her strength.

My S.M.U. experience was a succession of miracles. At age 16, I was the greenest freshman who ever enrolled—having a tuition scholarship, $50 (which my mother borrowed), and the promise of a job. At this juncture, my faith journey was reinforced yet again. Individuals such as Paul Scott, who not so incidentally was an ardent Christian Scientist, gave me a job at the Haskell Theatre in East Dallas. Dean of Men A. C. Zumbrunnen gave me incredible, often unsolicited, support even after I left S.M.U. He and Paul Scott were practicing Christians who somehow, with God's guidance, gave me the full benefit of their faith, however undeserving I might have been.

Another S.M.U. blessing came unexpectedly. I graduated in four years in 1932, but planned to return the following year to be editor of the student newspaper, *The Campus*, understandable in view of my journalism major. Dr. Shuler, Dean of the Graduate School, stopped me on the campus one day just before I graduated to inquire what my plans were, other than being editor, for the following school year. When I replied that I had no other plans, he invited me to his office, where he offered me an Arnold Fellowship in Government which, of course, I accepted, even though my government professors had never mentioned that to me. The result was that, at age 21, in August 1933, I left S.M.U. with the MA degree, which probably was worth more to me than a PhD would be today.

The next four years can best be described as my "wilderness" experience. Travel, excitement, girlfriends (none serious), time to ponder career possibilities, but all in the growing shadow of a war-threatened Europe. I was simply existing, going nowhere, not even to church, except when visiting my mother. Then, in the summer of 1937, at the nadir of my adult life, while working in the East Texas oil field, another miracle came. S.M.U. Dean Zumbrunnen received a phone call from the U.T.–Austin Dean of Students, V. I.

Moore, inquiring after my whereabouts. Moore wanted to offer me the job I had interviewed for more than three years earlier. When he called, I quickly accepted his offer, reporting for work as Assistant Dean of Student Life, U.T. Austin, in September 1937. My salary for nine months was $1500, but I would have worked for nothing to get my foot in that career door.

God truly works wonders. After one hour on the job, on September 8, 1937, I was introduced to Billy Ruth Young. Fifteen months later we were married. She was a staunch, life-long Methodist; after the usual "compromise," I became one. Sunday worship, as well as related church activities (especially with other young couples) became ritual for us.

On September 1, 1939, war erupted in Europe. One year later, I applied to join the U.S. Naval Reserve. In the summer of 1941, still employed at U.T. Austin and with half the academic work for a PhD completed, I was called to active duty. After eighteen months in New Orleans, we were ordered abroad, because of my five years of Spanish study, first to Mexico, and then to Paraguay for the rest of the war. Our church opportunities waned, but never our Christian commitment. Never our resort to prayer.

Once out of the Navy, we lived in Corsicana, waiting for my appointment as a Foreign Service Officer, for which I had applied when the war ended. We were active in the First Methodist Church, including service on the board. One year later, when my appointment came through, we left for Bogotá, Colombia, where I was assigned as Political Officer in the Embassy. We had a rich and gratifying experience in a mission church in Colombia, where Protestants of all denominations met for Sunday School and worship. Our minister was a Presbyterian missionary. Before our transfer, we were on the committee that selected the first full-time pastor at the American Church in Mexico City. Our first two children were born during the war and we were determined to provide them with Christian upbringing through Sunday School.

Next came Washington and a marvelous three years at the Chevy Chase Methodist Church. During that time I had a rare but profound difference with my church. Of course, I was assigned to the State Department as a mid-level officer. President Truman decided to send an ambassador to the Vatican. I recall holding off for a month as a Board member the church's resolution against the U.S. sending a representative to the Vatican.

It was then, in 1950-51, that I met Abram Vereide and became active in International Christian Leadership, and the National Prayer Breakfasts. Vereide was instrumental in starting the Prayer Breakfasts in both the House of Representatives and the Senate. I recall the introduction of the marvelous hymn "How Great Thou Art," composed in 1951, at the Presidential Prayer Breakfast. It was sung by the famous Metropolitan Baritone star, Jerome Hines. It is still one of my favorites.

My next career move was to Madrid, Spain, where I became Director of the U.S. Economic Mission. Once again, God revealed his mysterious ways. Our two older children were ripe for Sunday School, as were the children of friends and diplomatic colleagues, but there was no American Church. What to do?? The Anglican priest at the British Embassy Church, where we visited to worship, came to our rescue. "You teach the children," he said, "and I will offer you space for that. I will play the organ and preach for you at 10:30, before the Anglican service at 11:00." How is that for demonstrating Christian love in action?

In 1956, we returned to Washington, where I was to become Assistant Secretary of State for Inter-American Affairs. We lived near the Metropolitan Memorial Methodist Church and worshipped there (as did Vice-President Nixon). The Senior Minister was Edward Latch, who was Chaplain to the U.S. Senate. Our social life was demanding and unceasing, with twenty Latin-American Ambassadors, plus those at the Organization of American States as my "clients." But we tried to put our faith first. It was a testing time in which the Lord never let us down. This was the period when I was closely associated with Dr. Milton Eisenhower, brother of the President and a truly marvelous person. I accompanied Nixon on his trip to South America in May 1958 and had to deal with the emergence of Fidel Castro. Never a dull moment. Never a moment without God's presence and guidance.

In 1960, I was appointed Ambassador to Argentina by President Eisenhower and, a few months later, reappointed by President Kennedy. The American Church in Buenos Aires, founded by the Methodists, became our center of worship there. The first Sunday we attended church we sat next to an attractive older woman who introduced herself as the granddaughter of one of the fifty American school teachers who were invited to Argentina in the late 1880s, by Argentine president Julio Roco. Prior to his Presidency, he had served as Argentine Ambassador to the United States and had been so impressed with our public schools that he invited fifty American women teachers to come to Argentina.

I recall the visit to Buenos Aires of John Bolton, of International Christian Leadership. He spoke at the Benjamin Franklin Library (over objections of some U.S. staff). I invited some Catholic priests to hear this lay businessman speak of his Christian faith.

On our return to the U.S., we were assigned to the Naval War College in Newport, Rhode Island, as State Department representative. The First Methodist Church there was a colonial white frame building in downtown Newport. The congregation was small but loyal, e.g. the members prepared the church suppers. One retired Admiral in Newport asked me for our church affiliation. When I replied "Methodist," he urged me for reasons of social standing to affiliate with the Episcopalian, Congregational, or Baptist Church. Of course, we ignored his advice, and found rich fellowship and fulfillment in that small church.

I'm almost finished. In August 1964, I opted for early retirement from the Foreign Service, and I returned to Dallas to become Vice-President of S.M.U. We attended this church the first time in late August, 1964, and the next Thursday joined the Mr. and Mrs. Class. I taught the Mr. and Mrs. Class for two years, and then was co-teacher with Ronnie Sleeth for another year. The rest is known to some of you. We have been involved in myriad church activities for thirty-three years. It would be no exaggeration to say that it has been the center of our lives. Our Christian faith has sustained us through good times and bad, through happy times and sad.

To say we learned to depend on the Lord would be an understatement. We still do. Ours is a classic example of having given up things we could not keep in order to gain those things in Christ we could not lose.

Seated: Angie Rubottom, Dick, Billy Ruth, Eleanor Odden; standing: John, Taylor, and Jay Rubottom

Rubottom's sister, Nancy Merle Lea; her husband, Willis; and their three children, Nancy, Richard and Robert.

Another "bridge hand vacation" with Billy Ruth's siblings and spouses. This photo was taken in Ruidoso, New Mexico.

Dick's other sister, Martha Frances Johnson, and husband, Ernest (back left), are pictured here with their children, Ernest, Jr., Beth, Dick, Joy, Jack, and Tim, and their grandchildren.

The family of origin, 2007.

All the Rubottoms' grandchildren: Robert, Jay, Sarina and (in front) Taylor.

At their indoor swimming pool in Dallas, with granddaughter Taylor.

The family gathered for Billy Ruth's 90th birthday in September 2007.

In San Diego in 1998, standing: Sarina, Robert, Eleanor, Dick, Allan Odden. seated: Billy Ruth, Allan's mother, Mabel Odden.

With grandson Jay Rubottom.

At Salado: cousins Taylor, Jay, and Sarina.

(left to right) John, Dick, Jay, and Rick Rubottom.

John, Angie and Taylor Rubottom with Dick and Billy Ruth. Austin, 2001.

The extended family visited the Rubottoms in Dallas.

Three generations of Rubottom men: John, Jay, Dick.

Jay graduates from high school, 1999.

Dick and Billy Ruth, their children and spouses and grandchildren. Austin, 2006.

Dick greets his first great-grandson, Micah, held here by Dick's grand-daughter Sarina Odden Meyer. Looking on is Sarina's husband, Brett Meyer.

Index

A

Achilles, Theodore, 153, 154
Acuna Anzorena, Guillermo, 177
AFL-CIO, 65, 66, 132
Agrarian Reform Act, 125
Aguilar, Raul, 238, 239
Alemann, Roberto, 181
Alliance for Progress, 178
Alsogaray, Alvaro, 173, 178, 179, 183
American Church, Buenos Aires, 285
American media, 78, 79
American Society of Newspaper Editors, 120
Anderson House, 202
Anderson, Charles, 259, 260
Annals of the American Academy of Political and Social Science, The, 193
Argentina, 31-32, 44, 100, 207; early settlement, 203-204; politics, 172, 177, 182, 183
Argentina State Oil Company (YPF), 205
Armour, Norman, 45
Arnold Fellowship in Government, 15, 17, 282
Asunción, Paraguay, v, 30, 31, 33
Austin, Texas, 22, 25

B

Babieri, Umberto, 235

Baker, Keith, 223
Barton, Robert, 212
Batista, Fulgencio, 102, 103, 106, 108, 109, 111, 112, 113, 114, 115, 117, 118, 120, 140, 153, 169, 222, 223
Battle of Salta, 204
Bay of Pigs, 104-106, 107, 131, 142
Beaulac, Willard L., 33, 45, 46, 48
Beaulac, Mrs. Willard, 54
Beers, Beth, 251
Belgrano, Manuel, 204
Betancourt Bello, Rómulo Ernesto, 135, 140-141
Birnbaum, Maurice, 148, 149, 153
Blake, Bruce, 243
Bogotá, Colombia, 37, 38; riot and revolution, 47-49, 52-54
Bolton, John, 285
Bonsel, Phil, 124
Borges, Jorge Luis, 174
Boy Scouts of America, vii, 236, 270, 273; Silver Beaver Award, 252; Silver Buffalo Award, 252
Bracero Agreement, vi, 62-63, 65, 66, 67,68
Brooks, James, 230
Brownwood, Texas, 8
Burford, Jerry, 243
Bush, George H. W., 273

293

C

Cabot, John Moors, 91
Campaign of the Desert, 203
Campos, Ernesto M., 205
Campus, The, 282
Caracas, Venezuela, 149, 150, 154-157
Caracas, Declaration of 1954, 135
Caracas Resolution, 130
Carnegie Museum, 6
Carnegie Tech (Carnegie Mellon), 7
Carter, Darrell, 259, 260, 261
Carter, Pat, 45, 50, 51
Castro, Fidel, 103, 105, 108, 109, 115, 120, 124, 125, 127, 129, 134, 135, 136, 137, 140, 141, 153, 178, 179, 221, 222, 223
Castro, Raul, 103
CBS World Roundup, 202
Central Intelligence Agency (CIA), 98, 108, 117, 118, 119, 126, 127, 128, 138, 142
Central Methodist College, 257
Chamber of Commerce of U.S. in Argentina, 181-182, 183
Chambers, Whitaker, 146
Chamizal dispute, 60-61
Chevy Chase Methodist Church, 283
Chicago Tribune, 120
Christ Without Myth, 225
Clarin, 183
Clements, William P., 246, 252
Colborn, Page, 21
Colombia, political system, 47
Columbia University, 255
Commodoro Rivadavia, 203
Communism/Communist, 48, 51, 54, 79, 84, 90, 192, 193, 105, 108, 122, 125, 127, 129, 130, 134, 135, 151, 153, 169, 170, 190, 222, 223, 224, 225
Consular Corps of Dallas, 265
Contender, The, 145
Correo de la Tarde, 183
Corsicana Daily Sun, 55
Corsicana, Texas, 34

Council on Foreign Relations (Dallas), 265
Cross and Crescent, 237
Cross-Roads Project of the Greater Dallas Community of Churches, 240, 243
Cuba and the US, 141-142; and sugar legislation, 126
Cuban Missile Crisis, 106, 107, 142, 190

D

Daily Worker, The, 224
Dallas, 264
Dallas, Texas, Committee on Foreign Visitors, 260; Council on World Affairs, vii, 252, 260, 271; international visitors, 258, 259, 260, 262; Office of International Affairs, vii, 258, 259, 265; Office of Protocol, 258, 259; World Salute, 265, 269
Dallas Chamber of Commerce, 259, 260
Dallas Morning News, 79, 87, 258
David, Lewis, 230, 231
David, Mary Jo, 230, 231, 242
DeGarmo, Sharon, 262, 265
del Valle, Carlos Peon, 50, 51
Detroit Council of Foreign Relations, 70
"Development of United States Foreign Policy," 82
Dignan, Lolis Longoria, 261, 262, 263, 264
District Intelligence Headquarters, v
Dominican Republic, 139-140
Donnelly, Walter, 132
Douglas, Helen Gahagan, 146
Dreier, John, 45
Dubois, Jules, 120, 122
Dulles, Allen W., 98, 117, 119, 128, 131, 136, 142
Dulles, John Foster, 94, 96, 98, 111, 114, 130, 131, 135, 143, 144, 146, 162, 202
Dunn, James Plymouth, 79

E

Eastern Banker, 222
Economic Aid Program, 85
Eddy, Mary Baker, Scientific
  Statement of Being, 215
8th Naval District Intelligence, v, 28
Eisenhower, Dwight D., 94, 97,
  107, 115, 119, 120, 131, 138,
  142, 145, 146, 156, 162, 165,
  166, 170, 178, 197, 200, 201,
  202, 285
Eisenhower, John, 115
Eisenhower, Milton, 94, 127, 132,
  143, 144, 150, 285
Eliot, Anna Mae, 230, 231, 242
Eliot, George, 230, 231
Elizabethtown Hospital, 245
Export-Import Bank, 44

F

Falange, 83
First Methodist Church, Corsicana,
  24
First Methodist Church, Newport,
  285
Ford, Logan, 14
Ford, Mrs. Edsel, 201
Foreign Service ranks, 37
Fourth Floor, The, 111
Franco, Francisco, 74, 83, 85
Frigerio, Rogelio, 173, 177, 178,
  179, 180, 181, 182, 183
Frondizi, Arturo, 148, 152, 172,
  173, 174, 177, 178, 179, 180,
  181, 182, 184, 185, 190
Frondizi, Señora, 211
futbol, 79, 80, 89

G

Gaitán, Jorge Eliécer, 53; assassina-
  tion and riot, 47-48, 58
Garcia, Eduardo, 183
Gardner, Arthur, 111, 112
Gates, John, 224
Gellman, Irwin F., 145
Good Neighbor Commission of
  Texas, 252
Great Depression, 18

H

Guevara, Ernesto "Che," 103, 180,
  182; Goodwin-Guevara meeting,
  183
Guiberson Corporation, 22

H. Neil Mallon Award for Dis-
  tinguished Civic Service, 252, 271
Hackett, Charles Wilson, 27
Hamilton Park United Methodist
  Church, 241, 243
Hands Across the Border, 232
Harper's, 83
Harriman, Averell, 45, 50
Haskell Theatre, 282
Healy, George, 121
Herter, Christian A., 98, 127, 135,
  136, 146, 162, 223, 224
Hesburgh Commission, 66
Hesburgh, Theodore, 66
Highland Park United Methodist
  Church, vii, 240, 241, 256,
  278, 280
Hines, Jerome, 284
Hispanidad Program in Spain, 77
Hiss, Alger, 146
Hitler, Adolf, 75, 84
Hollamby, David, 264
Holland, Henry F., 91, 94, 97
Holland, Kenneth, 132
Hopkins, Jim, 277
Hotel Alfonso Treci, 124
House Un-American Activities
  Committee, 146
Houston Post, 162-163
Howard Payne College, 3, 4, 5, 11,
  203, 280
Hunt, H. L., 224

I

Ibanez del Campo, Carlos, 149
Industrial Advisory Committee,
  248
Inter-American Advisory
  Commission, 131, 143
Inter-American Bank, 137
Inter-American Business Center,
  250

Inter-American Conference of
American States, 42
Inter-American Defense Board, 139
Inter-American Development Bank,
100, 101
International Christian Leadership,
284, 285
International Institute for
Education, 132
International Monetary Fund (IMF),
84, 137
Item, 120

J
Jenkins Foundation, 248
John Birch Society, 222
Johnson, Lyndon B., 66, 165, 217
Johnson, Martha Frances, and fam-
ily, 6, 230, 288
Joint U.S.–Mexican Boundary and
Water Commission, 67
Junior League of Dallas, 259, 262,
263

K
KDKA, 6
Kelley, Chris, 258
Kennedy, Edward, 174
Kennedy, John F., 105, 131, 142,
165, 178, 179, 181, 184, 185,
217, 220, 285
Kilgore, Texas, 22; Rangerettes, 265
King, J. C., 143
Kingsville, Texas, 5
Kleberg Bank, 5
Knight, Jack, 132
Knit-wits, 246

L
La Prensa, 182, 183
La Violencia, 58
Lambda Chi Alpha, 13, 14, 18,
19, 20, 237, 238, 250
Landon School, 93
Latch, Edward, 284
Laurel Race Track, 201
Lea, Nancy Merle, and family, 6,
87, 89, 230, 251, 263, 287

"League of Nations and the
Codification of International
Law," 18
Leavey, General and Mrs., 201
Leddy, Ray, 70
Lee, Robert E., 211
Lewis, Fulton, 117
Life Magazine, 132
Lively, Earl, 222
Lockwood, Charles, 10
Lockwood, Etha, 10
Lockwood, Harold, 10
Lockwood, Maureen, 10
Lodge, John Davis, 79
Lord's Prayer, The, 1, 35
Lower Colorado River Authority
(LCRA), 256
Lozano Díaz, Julio, 102
Luter, John, 107, 148

M
Machado, Gerardo, 119, 169
Madeira School, 93
Madrid, Spain, 74, 79, 199
Magloire, Paul, 102
Mallon, Ann, 271
Mann, Thomas, 61, 126
Manning, Bayless, 177
Manrique, Francisco, 183
Manzanillo, Mexico, v, 29
Marble Collegiate Church, 198
Marshall, George C., 43, 45, 50,
51, 54, 58, 129, 162
Marshall Plan, 146
Mathews, Herbert, 122
Matiauda, Alfredo Stroessner, 152
Matthews, Herbert, 83, 109, 110,
111
McCall, Parkhurst & Horton, 256
McKie, Steve, 10
Meacham, J. Lloyd, 27
Menendez Behety family, 203,
205, 210
Metropolitan Memorial Methodist
Church, 284
Mexico, Lend-Lease Agreement,
71
Meyer, Brett, 292

Meyer, Charles, 131
Meyer, Micah, 292
Meyer, Sarina Odden, 255, 288, 289, 290, 292
Mikoyan, Anastas Hovhannesi, 134
Miller, Herb and Kay, 242
Miller, Mr. and Mrs. M. M., 18-19, 234
Mola, Emilio, 74
Montevideo, Uruguay, 42, 150, 151, 152, 166, 169
Moore, V. I., 20, 22, 25, 283
Morinigo, Higinio, 33
Mr. and Mrs. Class, 286
Munro, Dana, 132
Murphy, Franklin, 277
Murphy, J. Carter, 74, 228
Murphy, Richard W., 128
Murphy, Robert, 131, 136, 157

N
Nagle, Fred, 230
Nagle, Tillie Frances, 230, 242
Narden, Maebelle, 53
Nasser, Gamal Abdel, 86
National Civil Service League Citation, 252
National Prayer Breakfasts, 284
National Youth Administration (NYA), 25
NATO treaty, 129
Naval Station Rota, Spain, 86
Naval War College Review, The, 193
Naval War College, 192, 194, 195, 235, 285
New Orleans, Louisiana, 28
New York Herald Tribune, 79
New York Times, 79, 83, 109, 110, 111, 132
Nixon, Pat, 150, 154, 156, 167
Nixon, Richard, 145-146, 147, 148, 162, 164-167, 169, 172, 266, 284, 285; trip to South America, 146-160
Noticias Graficas, 183
Nowotny, Shorty, 23, 25

O
O'Dwyer, William, 165
O'Rourke, John, 104, 120
Odden, Allan, 244, 255, 278, 289
Odden, Eleanor Rubottom, 20, 29, 31, 56, 69, 80, 93, 170, 188, 192, 195, 198, 199, 200, 201, 202, 211, 234, 244, 246, 255, 278, 287, 288, 289
Odden, Mabel, 289
Odden, Robert Allan Myung Soo, 255, 288, 289
Odden , Sarina, *see* Sarina Meyer
Odría, Manuel, 103
Ogden, Shubert, 225
Organization of American States (OAS), 51, 55, 58, 97, 100, 104, 122, 129, 136, 137, 139, 141
Ospina, Mariano, 47, 49
Owens Foundation, 252

P
Pact of Madrid, 77, 78, 79
Pan American Oil Company, 203
Pan American Union, 58, 202
Paraguay revolution, 33
Paridad, 47
Pawley, William, 45, 117, 118, 119, 134
Payne, Edward Howard, 3
Peale, Norman Vincent, 198
Pecan Valley Baptist Association, 3
Pembroke, 188
PEMEX, 29
Pérez Jiménez, Marcos Evangelista, 101, 135, 136, 149
Perkins School of Theology, 225
Perón, Juan, 102, 103, 152, 172, 204
Peronists, 152, 173, 177, 178, 190
Phillip, Duke of Edinburgh, 201
Phillips Exeter Academy, 80, 93, 188
Pinilla, Rojas, 47, 102
Pittsburgh Pirates, 7

Pittsburgh, Pennsylvania, 6
Prado Museum, 201
Presbyterian Hospital (Dallas), 246
Prieto, Renee, 277
Prince Charles, 264, 265
Pruett, George W., 280
Punta del Este Conference, 183

Q
Queen Elizabeth, 201
Quintanilla, Luis, 50

R
Radical Civic Union, 152
Ragland Department Store, 5
Reagan, Ronald, 66
Red Star Over Cuba, 133
Rhodes, Loab, 203
Richardson (Texas) *Digest*, 222
Richardson, Bill, 277
Richmond, Dr., 198
Rio Grande City, 203, 205, 206, 208, 210
Rio Grande River, 60, 67, 163, 206, 209
Rio Treaty, 129, 134, 135
Roa, Raul, 136, 137, 138
Roca, General, 203
Roco, Julio, 285
Roosevelt, Franklin D., 165
Rotary Club of Dallas, 237, 238
Rotary Clubs, 251
Round Rock, Texas, 27
Rubottom, Angela Jane Taylor, 256, 278, 287, 291
Rubottom, Billy Ruth, v, vi, vii, 20, 22-23, 25, 29, 31, 46, 56, 68, 188, 218, 227, 228, 230, 232, 233-235, 241, 242, 244, 245, 246, 247, 251, 254, 256, 263, 279, 283, 287, 289, 291, 292; correspondence, 39, 41, 52-54, 55, 56-57, 62, 69
Rubottom, Eleanor Ann, *see* Eleanor Rubottom Odden
Rubottom, Jennie Eleanor Watkins 4-5, 8, 9, 19, 280
Rubottom, John William, 72, 170, 195, 197, 198, 199, 202, 219, 227, 234, 244, 247, 256, 278, 287, 288, 290, 291
Rubottom, Jr., John William "Jay," 256, 287, 288, 289, 290, 291
Rubottom, Lynn Thompson, 256
Rubottom, Martha Frances, *see* Martha Frances Johnson
Rubottom, Nancy Merle, *see* Lea, Nancy Merle
Rubottom, Richard "Rick," 20, 31, 56, 69, 93, 170, 188, 192, 195, 198, 199, 200, 201, 202, 211, 234, 255, 256, 278, 288, 290
Rubottom, Jr., Roy Richard:
accident, 244-247
advisor to Governor Bill Clements, vii, 252
Assistant Secretary of State for Inter-American Affairs, vi, 91, 94, 97, 98, 99
awards, 71, 252
birth, 5
career service, Ambassador to Argentina, vi, 93, 104, 170, 171, 172, 178, 185-190; assigned to Colombia, 37-59, Mexico, 29-30, Paraguay, 30-34, Spain, 74-90, Washington, D.C., 60-73; beginning, v, vi; Career Minister, 220; Counselor of the Embassy for Economic Affairs, 89; First Secretary of Embassy, 74
correspondence, 160, 161, 162, 196-214, 278
Dallas Council of World Affairs, 252, 260, 271
Deputy/Director of Mexican Affairs, vi, 60, 63, 65, 68
Director of Dallas Office of International Affairs, vi, 258, 259, 265
Director of U.S. Operations Mission, 75, 89
Diplomat in Residence of World Cruise, 254

education/school, 27; classical music training, 6; desegregated schools, 6; high school graduation, 10; learning Spanish, v; M.A. degree, 17; master's, 15, 17, 18

Ethics Committee of Texas Bar Association, vii

faith/religion, viii, 240, 243, 280-281; personal affirmations, viii, 1, 35, 215, 247, 275, 279

family/relatives, 9, 69, 81, 230

foreign policy outlook, 75-77

Grievance Committee, 6th District, State of Texas, 239, 240, 253

honorary doctorates, 238, 257

Lambda Chi Alpha, vii, 237, 238; Grand High Zeta, 237

marriage, 23-24, 25-27; 50th wedding anniversary, 267, 268

military service, 28; Naval Attaché, vi, 30, 31; Naval Commission, v; Naval Liaison Officer, 29; U.S. Naval War College, 185, 186, 188, 192-195

on Cuba, 107-144

on education, 80

President of the University of the Americas, 248, 250, 251, 252

retirement, vi, 218-220

Rotary Club of Dallas, 237

at SMU, Assistant Dean of Student Life, 283; controversy, 221-225; editor of newspaper, 15; interim president, 232; professor emeritus, 252; retirement from, 252; value to, 228; Vice-President for Administration, 227, 228; Vice-President for University Life, 213, 221

wages, 39, 93

work/work ethic, 7, 9, 12, 13, 21, 266

Rubottom, Sr., Roy Richard, 5, 6, 7, 8, 9, 19, 20, 280

Rubottom, Taylor Elizabeth, 256, 278, 287, 288, 290, 291

Rubottom family, children's education, 41, 80, 92-93; extended family, 87; family reunion, 271, 230; friends, 80

Rusk, Dean, 162, 179, 186

S

Salta, Argentina, 204

San Jose Conference, 134

Santa Fe Railroad, 13

Schenley Hotel, 7

Scott, Paul, 12, 282

Security National Bank, 6

Sevilla-Sacasa, Guillermo, 171

Shelton, Dr., 280, 281

Sherman, Forrest P., 85

Shuler, Dr., 282

Silver Spring, Maryland, 69

Six Crises, The, 153, 166

Sleeth, Ronnie, 286

Smith, Earl E. T., 111, 112, 113, 114, 123, 124, 133

Snow, Billy, 114

Somoza Garcia, Anastasio, 102

South Fork, 264

Southern Methodist University (SMU), 10, 11, 12, 218, 221-229, 248, 252, 286; Distinguished Alumnus, 252; and free speech, 224, 225; Ibero American Civilization Department, 261; and liberalism, 222; Master Plan and committee, 227-228, 230; and student unrest in 1960s, 228-229

Southwestern College, 238

Spain and the United States since World War II, 74, 77

Spain, economy, 89-90; political history, 82-84; U.S. relationship, 74, 75, 77, 78, 82-87

Spanish Royalists, 204

Sparks, Ambassador, 167

SS Brazil, 186

Stagecoach Inn, 230
State Bar Association (Minnesota), 239
State Bar Association (Texas), 239, 253
State National Bank, 34
Stevenson, Adlai, 179
Strategic Intelligence School, 80
Strauss, Annette, 269
Summit at Lakeway, 279

T

Taft-Hartley Act, 146
Tate, Willis, 18, 218, 221, 224, 225, 226, 227, 228, 229, 232, 248
Taylor, Starke, 259
Tennessee Gas & Oil, 205
Terry, Marshall, 221, 224-225, 227
The Forum, 278, 279
Tierra del Fuego, 203, 205, 206
Time, 83, 132, 177-178
Times Picayune, 120
Tower, John, 270
Toynbee, Arnold, 211
Trujillo, Rafael, 101-102, 108, 140, 141, 153
Truman, Harry S., 66, 71, 165, 284
23rd Psalm, 275

U

U.S. Agency for International Development, 250
U.S. and Cuba, 103-106, 125, 128, 180, 183
U.S. and Latin America, 44, 159
U.S. Information Service, 159
U.S. Naval Reserve, 283
University Afloat, 254
University of Montevideo, 151
University of San Marcos, 153, 160
University of the Americas, 248, 250, 252
Uruguay, 150

V

Varney, Harold Lord, 222
Venezuela, 135, 149, 150; trade agreement, 68, 70, 71
Vereide, Abram, 284
Voice of America, 159
Voorhis, Jerry, 145

W

War Manpower Act, 34
Washington Daily News, 104, 120
Washington Post, 79
Washington Times, 277
Watergate, 162
Watkins, Jennie Eleanor, *see* Jennie Eleanor Rubottom
Watkins, Martha, 281
Watkins, W. D., 3-4, 9, 12, 13, 281
Western Hemisphere Governance, 252
Westinghouse Turbine Repair Center, 256
Weyl, Nathaniel, 223
Wichita Falls, Texas, 5, 6
Wild, Nathaniel, 133
Wine Is Bitter, The, 94, 150
Woodward, Robert, 151
World Affairs Council of Dallas, 265
World Bank, 84

Y-Z

Yale Law School, 177
Young, Billy Ruth, *see* Billy Ruth Rubottom
Young, Eleanor, 230, 231
Young, Jack R., 213
Young, Maurice, 230, 231, 242
Zumbrunnen, A. C., 22, 282